Out of the Depths
I Call to You

Queſta תְּפִלָּה dee dirſi dalla Donna la pri

ma volta che porge il Latte al ſuo

Fanciullino.

יְהִי רָצוֹן מִלְפָנֶיךָ יְיָ אֱלֹקַי וֵאלֹקֵי

אֲבוֹתַי שֶׁתְּזַמִין מָזוֹן עֲבֶדֶךָ

הַתִינוֹק הַזֶה בְּרַבּוּי חָלָב דֵי מַחְסוֹרוֹ

אֲשֶׁר יֶחְסַר לוֹ. וְתָשִׂים בְּלִבִּי הָעֵת

שֶׁצָרִיךְ לְהָנִיקֵהוּ כְּדֵי לָתֵת לָהּ לוֹ.

וְהָקֵל מֵעָלַי הַשֵׁנָה וּבְעֵת שֶׁיִבְכֶּה

פָּתַח אָזְנַי כְּדֵי לִשְׁמוֹעַ מִיָד

וְהַצִילֵנִי שֶׁלֹא תִפּוֹל יָדִי עָלָיו בְּעֵת

הַשֵׁנָה וְיָמוּת חַס וְשָׁלוֹם. וְיִהְיוּ לְרָצוֹן

אִמְרֵי פִי וְהֶגְיוֹן לִבִי לְפָנֶיךָ יְיָ צוּרִי וְגוֹאֲלִי

Out of the Depths I Call to You

A Book of Prayers for the Married Jewish Woman

EDITED AND TRANSLATED BY

Rabbi Nina Beth Cardin

A book of prayers for the married woman, specifically to be used on the occasions of her monthly cycle; upon removing the *hallah*; upon lighting the Shabbat and holiday candles; and at the time of her pregnancy, childbirth, and recovery. Written in the year 5546 (1786) for Mrs. Yehudit Kutscher Coen.

Jason Aronson Inc.
Northvale, New Jersey
London

The author gratefully acknowledges permission to reprint the following:

Translations of psalms from *Siddur Sim Shalom*, edited with translations, by Rabbi Jules Harlow. Published by the Rabbinical Assembly and the United Synagogue of America. Copyright © 1985 by the Rabbinical Assembly. Reprinted by permission.

Original Hebrew and Italian pages from Mss. Mic. nos. 4290, 4322, 4371, 4333B, 4375, 4336. Courtesy of the Library of the Jewish Theological Seminary of America.

Excerpts of translations from the *Tanakh*, reprinted with permission of the Jewish Publication Society.

Library of Congress Cataloging-in-Publication Data

Seder tefilot nidah, halah, hadlakah. English & Hebrew.
    Out of the depths I call to you : a book of prayers for the
married Jewish woman / [edited and translated by] Nina Beth Cardin.
      p. cm.
    Contains Hebrew text of Seder tefilot nidah, halah, hadlakah,
presented by Giuseppe Coen to his wife in 1786, with introduction
and translation in English.
    "The book is a composite of psalms, blessings, and personal
prayers divided into topical sections, each section punctuated with
Italian directions . . . instructing the petitioner in the proper use
of the prayers"—Introd.
    ISBN 0-87668-600-5
    1. Woman, Jewish—Prayer-books and devotions—Hebrew. 2. Women,
Jewish—Prayer-books and devotions—English. 3. Judaism—Prayer-
books and devotions—Hebrew. 4. Judaism—Prayer-books and
devotions—English. 5. Manuscripts, Hebrew—New York (N.Y.)—
Facsimiles. 6. Jewish Theological Seminary of America. Library.
I. Cardin, Nina Beth. II. Coen, Giuseppe. III. Jewish Theological
Seminary of America. Library. Seder tefilot nidah, halah,
hadlakah. IV. Title.
BM667.W6S413 1991
296.7'2'024042—dc20   91-15950
                                                      CIP
                                                      HE

Manufactured in the United States of America. Jason Aronson Inc. offers books and cassettes. For information and catalog write to Jason Aronson Inc., 230 Livingston Street, Northvale, New Jersey 07647.

Contents

Acknowledgment

Every book is in some way a gift from the author to the anonymous reader. It is given in the hope that the reader shares the author's joy in exploration and her excitement of new discoveries. And in truth, this book is my gift to you, but it is also a gift to those who first recited the prayers found here, those who turned to these prayers in their most private of moments, those we call our mothers. It is a gift that tells them that they and their ways have not been silenced and have not been forgotten.

Recapturing lost traditions is an essential task for the modern Jewish woman for it is only by including women in the history and legacies of Judaism that the fullness of our tradition can be witnessed, understood, and ultimately experienced. This book is a most modest effort to contribute to a holy task.

I have been aided in this precious work by a host of generous people. Indeed, the idea of sharing my interests and discoveries with a reading public was first given to me too many years ago by my dear but distant friend, Rabbi Martin Cohen. I would not be surprised if he believed his early proddings and encouragement had all been for nought. But look, Martin, I have begun.

I thank also the many groups and classes I have taught and with whom I shared this material. Their enthusiasm and questions helped me to continue deeper and deeper investigations into what these texts might have meant to the women who recited them.

I thank *Lilith* magazine for publishing my first translations and bringing me to the attention of Mr. Arthur Kurzweil at Jason Aronson Publishers. Were it not for Mr. Kurzweil's support for this project, this book might never have seen the light of day.

Dr. Raymond Scheindlin of the Jewish Theological Seminary graciously agreed to read passages of the manuscript, pale in comparison with his masterpieces, and offered invaluable comments and criticism. How can one repay another for the greatest gift of all, their time?

I thank Ms. Diane Troderman for her unflagging belief in this project, the wonderful discussions we have had, and her careful reading of sections of the manuscript.

Mr. Francesco Melfi helped me selflessly with the translation of the Italian. I cannot thank him enough for his patience, precision, kindness, and generosity of time.

Ms. Karen Aiello was a true partner in the book's production, carefully preparing draft after draft after draft of the manuscript and serving as a most welcome, discerning audience.

Mr. Hector Guzman joined the project near its end. He carefully and deliberately saw to all the details necessary in getting the manuscript to the publisher.

I thank the Library of the Jewish Theological Seminary of America for allowing me to reproduce this manuscript from their Rare Book and Manuscript Collection, and Rabbi Michael Monson of the Jewish Publication Society and Rabbi Jules Harlow of the Rabbinical Assembly for allowing me to reprint translations of the psalms.

I offer my sincerest thanks to all those who contributed to the genesis, concept, creation, and production of this book.

Most of all, I thank my family: my father and mother who are unceasing sources of encouragement and support; my children, Etan, Elnatan, Noam, and Ateret (the latter two whose births were accompanied by the recitation of segments from this text) for allowing me to take time from their unreplenishable childhood to fulfill this dream; and most of all to my husband, who helped me with the crafting of difficult translations, who listened patiently as I read the entire manuscript to him aloud (not all at one sitting) to be sure it sounded the way I wanted, and who always, always is there for me.

May the work that I have produced find favor in God's eyes.

Introduction

In 1786 Dr. Giuseppe Coen presented his bride of two years with a very special gift: a book of prayers dedicated to her. The book was 112 pages long, 7⅛ inches high, and 4⅞ inches wide. It was bound in highly worked green leather and imprinted with gold on its front, back, and spine. But unlike other prayer books that contain mostly communal prayers whose recitation is governed by the Jewish calendar, this book was filled with private prayers, whose recitation was largely determined by a woman's biological calendar. Not surprisingly, the book contained prayers to be said upon preparing bread (*hallah*) and upon lighting the Shabbat candles, two of the three commandments pointedly assigned to women. But mostly it offered prayers to be said upon the events surrounding a Jewish woman's journey from wife to mother. Such events include the *mitzvah* of *mikveh* (the ritual bath—the third of the "women's commandments"), pregnancy, childbirth, delivery, nursing, and recovery. Written in Hebrew and calligraphed by an artistic hand, the book was passed from generation to generation until it found a home in the Rare Book Room of the Library of the Jewish Theological Seminary of America.

The book is a composite of psalms, blessings, and personal prayers divided into three topical sections, each section set apart by directions in Italian and an occasional Hebrew term, instructing the petitioner in the proper use of the prayers.

The first two sections—on *hallah* and candlelighting—are predominantly composed of biblical passages, mostly from the Book of Psalms. There is no need for heavy-handed personal petitions here. The *hallah* is taken, the candles are lit, and life goes on. However, not eager to pass up an opportunity to engage God in conversation, the petitioner places before God general, all-purpose supplications for health and well-being, both for her family and all Israel. In the final section, encompassing *mikveh* to parturition, there are many personal compositions focusing on herself and her single-minded goal to conceive and bear a child. Lengthy biblical quotations recede while biblical phrases, allusions, and characters, as well as *midrashim* based upon them, shape every petition.

The intensity and tension build on the evening the woman goes to *mikveh*, from the moment she leaves her home until she prepares to reenter the marriage bed. We do not see the grief, the disappointment (or perhaps the relief?) the woman experiences should her efforts not result in conception. The prayer book picks up in earnest once the woman has conceived. Different prayers then mark the different stages of her pregnancy. The tone becomes ever more personal, ever more earnest, ever more urgent as the woman moves through the first days of pregnancy, to the ninth month, to the birthing bed.

This is a book for when things go right. There are no prayers here to heal one's soul after miscarriage; no prayers here offering comfort when the relentless, heartless monthly stain of infertility comes once again; no prayers to mourn a stillbirth. While this may be a book for a newlywed, or a mother of two, it may not be a book that speaks to the mother of seven. This is a book for those women who want to have children, who approach the idea with trepidation and desire, and who ultimately succeed. It must be accepted on its own terms.

Composition

From the moment this book is opened, the reader is confronted with many questions. Who wrote the book? Why? How old are the prayers? Were they written by one author? If not, when did they first appear in one volume? Was the original language of composition Hebrew or are these prayers a translation? Did Yehudit Kutscher Coen really use this book? Did it speak to her needs?

In a subscript on the title page, written in Italian, in a hand different from the book's scribe, we read that Giuseppe Coen himself penned the book for his wife. Indeed, the book is personalized, for certain prayers include his wife's name (albeit in small letters, p. 63). The volume clearly was created for her. However, the prayers appear to be generic. The fact that her name is written in smaller letters indicates that it is *formulaic* for the petitioner, any petitioner, to insert her own name here. The tone of the directions introducing the prayers is likewise formulaic and impersonal ("Every woman says . . .). Although the book was *penned* expressly for Yehudit Kutscher Coen (Baila Yudita bat Rahel), the prayers have been borrowed.

This prayer genre was seemingly popular in the eighteenth century. Fragments of several other Italian *siddurim* for women, some with almost identical prayers and comparable instructions (both in Hebrew and Italian), can be found in the Jewish Theological Seminary's Rare Book Room and are known to exist elsewhere, both in private hands and public collections. In these various books, in the place where the petitioner's name is to be inserted, we find either a personal name, usually written by a hand other than the book's calligrapher, or even more interestingly, the generic "so and so, daughter of so and so." Whereas many of the extant books were written for a particular owner, some were clearly created for sale on the open market.

Helping us to understand both the nature and content of the book translated here, Dr. Coen (if our anonymous informant as to who wrote the book is correct) tells us, at the end of his volume, how the book came into being. "When I first considered writing this book, I was desirous of including in it the many incantations, charms, protective phrases, and vows that ease the burden of labor [in childbirth] and that I learned from our ancestors, and our books and writings." But, he goes on to say, he was mindful of the fact that the Ari (Isaac Luria, one of the most influential of kabbalists, 1534–1572) warned that the improper use of these prayers often causes miscarriage or premature birth. And the one who causes such loss is culpable and must fast ninety days. Therefore, the editor refrained from passing on this powerful information.

Despite the appearance of some superstitious behavior prescribed in the book, such as reciting biblical verses both forward and backward and repeating phrases three times, the author/editor/writer was quite restrained in this area. Whether it was really because of fear of the misuse of magical powers or, quite the contrary, the beginning of disinclination to promote superstitious beliefs—as may be hinted at in the book—we do not know. We know only that some of the prayers are based on those from the Ari, and others that could have been included were not.

On the last pages of the book, Dr. Coen gives us a glimpse of these powerful, excised incantations. In a section called *Tefillah Nora'ah* (The Awesome Prayer), the editor addresses the person (grammatically, a male) who is attending a woman in childbirth. The editor presents Psalm 20 (which is to be recited twelve times, each time concentrating on one of the twelve letters of God's divine names), with two notable changes. First, each time God's name (YHVH) appears, it is written with the vowels from a different phrase to be recalled during the recitation of the psalm. Kabbalistic powers are therefore invoked throughout. Second, grammatically, the psalm in the Bible is addressed to a male; in this *siddur*, it is addressed to the woman in labor. That is, instead of *Ya'ankha*, "May God answer you (masculine)," it is written *Ya'anekh*, "May God answer you (feminine)." Deliberately altering biblical texts is almost unheard of in tradition, although rare examples are found in the traditional liturgy. Changing a psalm's gender or voice is rarer still. But the awesome, numinous moment of birth alters the boundaries of propriety and admits women into the central circle of liturgy and ritual.

What was the language of composition? Many prayers within this book have woven within them words and phrases borrowed from the Bible (see, for example, pp. 73–77 or p. 99). Other prayers incorporate terms and language directly from the *siddur* (see the bottom of p. 61). Still others possess original poetic elements (p. 61), reinforcing the conjecture that the language of composition must have been Hebrew. The text is full of allusions to midrashic images and talmudic passages (see, for example, p. 65 and pp. 79–81). A fuller appreciation of the prayers emerges through a better understanding of the sources that inform them, some of which will be pointed out in the annotations throughout the book. Whether these references were familiar to the women of the *siddur* and hence enhanced their connectedness and resonance to the text, or whether the words did not go beyond the dimension presented on the page, we cannot know. Still, the beauty here, as in all good texts, is the multilayered engagement the reader can experience.

The last entry in the original manuscript claims that this collection of prayers is original. Most, if not all, of the prayers are borrowed, as we can see from the formality of the directions and comparable texts in other collections. However, beyond the question of the origin of these prayers is the question of distribution and usage of these prayers. Were they widespread and well known or available only to the privileged? Were these prayers truly spoken or kept respectfully on a shelf? Were they the author's imaginings of what a woman might say, or did these prayers speak compellingly to women's fears and desires? What compelled the author to compose the prayers? Did women memorize these prayers and speak them from the heart? Did they carry the book to and from the *mikveh* with them? Did women compose these prayers, or did men? How we answer these questions will determine whether we view these prayers as polemics written by men for women, hence reflecting a traditional (patriarchal) Jewish hermeneutic, or whether these prayers, regard-less of authorship, provide us with a clear window into the world of eighteenth-century Jewish women's spiritual lives.

We may never learn the answers to all these questions. Certainly, it is too early in the examination of this genre of literature to have the answers. Yet we can learn something from the few bits that have been examined. Yehudit Coen's prayer book may be the most elegant volume yet found, but it is not the only one. As already noted, other manuscripts from Italy are extant. Some are neat and attractive; others are coarse and unsophisticated. Some are personalized, embedding the petitioner's name in the prayers. Others are generic, writing "so and so" in the place of a name. Both types reveal the broader interest among women to own these collections, and presumably, recite these prayers. (It is important to know that no *printed* book of women's Hebrew prayers from this period has been discovered. Clearly, those who owned and ran the printing presses were not impressed with the need to mass produce such a book.) There is evidence that not only were these books used, but they were handed down from mother to daughter, one generation to the next. There is one prayer book in which a daughter apparently inherited her mother's book and wrote her own name (Olympia, daughter of) above her mother's name (Stella, daughter of Esther) in the body of the text.

Some of these prayer books were commissioned, some perhaps were copied by the women themselves, while other volumes were created for sale on the open market. The volume reproduced here has a genealogy record of the offspring of Yehudit and Giuseppe that shows that the book was kept in the family for almost 100 years. The front and back inside covers contain dates and brief narratives, in different hands, concerning the births and deaths of several Coen family members. More evidence about the use of these texts will no doubt come to light as more volumes are brought to light. Oral histories of women raised in the Italian-Jewish tradition may also illuminate the usage and role of these prayers.

The Significance of the Prayer Book

Yehudit Coen's was a most extravagant book. Not only was it marvelously penned and exquisitely bound, but it was a book that presented itself as a unit, a conceptual entity with beginning, middle, and end. Other less elegant Hebrew manuscripts of Italian women's prayers present themselves as a catalog of prayers more or less arranged in logical order. They are not self-referential. This manuscript, however, has a full title page, table of contents (which we moved to the front of the book), and indicators alerting the reader that she has come to the end of a section or series of prayers. On occasion, one section of the book would refer to another section. The move from a collection of prayers to an organic prayer book is subtle but substantial. Prayers are momentary. They address the occasion. Prayer books are integrative. They address the individual. They speak to more than the occasions within them. They speak to the person who experiences them all. Throughout this book, Baila Yudita bat Rahel (Yehudit Kutscher Coen) proves to be more than a woman with discrete religious needs. She is a religious woman. Dr. Coen may not have realized the importance of his creating a *book*. However, we can see here the literary beginnings of a different view of woman as Jew.

An orthographic peculiarity about this book is the way the word *God* is written. Instead of *Eloheinu*, it is written *Elokeinu*. (This is simply an orthographic technique. When reciting the prayers, the woman no doubt said *Eloheinu*.) The holiness of God's name demands that it be written in full only in bona fide biblical or liturgical texts. The substitution of " ק " for

xiii

" ה " is an accepted method of representing God's name in all other contexts. Does this spelling throw into doubt the perceived authoritativeness, that is, the perceived holiness, of this book? Not necessarily. A review of other similar prayer books reveals that while some substitute " ה " with " ק " or even " ד ," others spell out God's name in full. So perhaps another less disparaging explanation is that the scribe anticipated that this prayer book would accompany the woman into places and circumstances where sacred texts are generally forbidden. Therefore, the circumvention in writing God's name allows the book to travel where it must.

In addition to the prayers translated and annotated here, manuscript 4371 contains an additional 26 pages. Seventeen of those pages contain a traditional version of the *Shema* recited before going to bed, that can also be found in most contemporary prayer books. Three pages contain the Book of Jonah, placed at the end, as the book explains, for those who are wont to recite it in the presence of a woman in labor. Two pages contain an all-purpose incantation to ward off the Evil Eye. The remaining pages of the book contain the *Tefillah Nora'ah* (the Awesome Prayer), the author's end note, both described above, and two meditations created to help coax out the child aborning.

After the "Awesome Prayer," the person attending the laboring woman is told to lean over and whisper into the woman's ear: "*Pok. Pku. Upk. Ukp. Kpu. Kop.*" *Pok* in Aramaic means "get out" or "come out." These six permutations are meant to conjure a comprehensive sympathetic energy so the child will depart easily from its mother. Uttering every possible arrangement of the letters, the attendant leaves the baby no alternative.

The final liturgical act that can be performed to help the woman in labor, indeed the final ritual element described in the book, is an incantation that the editor believes to be a tradition that came from the ancients. It is to be recited when the baby is just about to be born, when the woman is lost in her cries of pain. Those attending her may choose to say, forward and backward three times: "Go forth from the ark, you and your wife; your sons and your sons' wives with you" (Genesis 8:15). The key elements here are the first three words, Go forth from the ark, צא מן התיבה . The ark is the womb and the child is being addressed, adjured to come out, with the very words God commanded Noah to leave the ark. Separation is necessary for life to begin. God created the world by separating light from darkness, waters from the waters, dry land from the seas. So life is continually created by separation. There are times to gather together, times to join. But bringing forth life—whether is it Noah from the ark or a child from its mother—requires separation. Using this verse also reminds us that this one child represents much more. Just as Noah, one individual, represented his family and indeed the future of the entire world, so each individual child represents generations of worlds to come.

A Note on the Translation

The translations of the biblical texts that appear in this book are drawn from two sources: *Tanakh: The Holy Scriptures* (the new Jewish Publication Society translation), and the Conservative movement's *Siddur Sim Shalom* daily prayer book, edited by Rabbi Jules Harlow.

Since the psalms in this book are to be used as liturgical pieces, that is, as poetry recited to affect and motivate both the one who reads and the One who hears, I selected those translations that best serve this purpose.

The translation of the petitionary prayers is my own. It is designed to reproduce the meaning, cadence, and feeling of the original text. For example, extensive repetitions found in the Hebrew, a common emphatic, almost mantric, style, have been maintained in the English. God-language remains masculine, allowing it to be an honest representation of the Hebrew and of the image most likely held by an Italian woman. Uses of "man," "he," and other such masculine referents in the psalms likewise have been largely (but not exclusively) retained, again because they are probably an honest representation of the Italian reader's understanding of the biblical text.

It should not surprise us that women of eighteenth-century Italy could read, and most likely write, both Hebrew and Italian. The Italian Jewish community was known for its commitment to formally educate both boys and girls. (Indeed, this period in Italian history saw the growth of a talented but generally unknown woman poet, Rachel Murporgo, who composed short works in Hebrew for family events and her own pleasure.)

The directions in this book reveal a little of what every educated Italian Jewish woman could have been expected to know and do. Several prayers, for example, are introduced by the directions, "To be recited every day after the *Sh'moneh Esrai* and before *Oseh Shalom*." (The *Sh'moneh Esrai*, or *Amidah*, is the silent prayer found at the center of each of the three daily services. The *Oseh Shalom* is the personal conclusion of the *Sh'moneh Esrai*.) Several assumptions are revealed here: (1) women prayed; (2) women prayed regularly, even daily; and (3) they recited much, if not most, of the traditionally established daily prayers. Clearly, this prayer book seems to have functioned as a supplement to other standard daily prayer books and prayer experiences that Italian women must have had. Indeed, such standard prayer books dating from the sixteenth century, commissioned for women and translated into Italian but written with Hebrew letters, are known to exist. A woman's ritual and religious life, then, was not merely relational, that is, limited to her role as wife and mother. Italian women were expected to have prayerful lives, only one part of which included prayers for the domestic sphere.

This area of women's prayers has been virtually ignored by scholars, male and female alike. Basic research, such as identifying sources and companion texts, still desperately needs to be pursued. This absence of research is most surprising, given the explosion of Jewish women's studies and the grassroots efforts worldwide to (re)create women's rituals. We can more authentically and authoritatively craft for the modern Jewish woman responses to religious moments, so egregiously overlooked in mainstream Judaism, if we search our mothers' past for their lost traditions. Whether we retrieve a usable past or whether we choose to reject what we find as not authentic for us, not speaking in our voice, we owe it to our ancestors to redeem them and their traditions from obscurity, and to understand them and their ways. Our first task then is simply to reveal, to uncover. Our second task is to understand. Our third is to analyze. Only lastly, after we have given them their due, can we measure them against the yardstick of our needs.

It is hoped that this book will be a beginning, an introduction, to the enterprise of unlocking and unfolding Jewish women's liturgical and ritual experiences. It is an effort to bring to the broader public a glimpse into a world not often imagined, or worse, not even missed.

Nina Beth Cardin

Out of the Depths
I Call to You

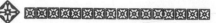

Prayers to Be Said on the Taking of *Hallah*

Before removing the hallah, *every woman recites the following prayer:*

A SONG of Ascent
Out of the depths I call to You;
Lord, hear my cry, heed my plea.

Attend to my prayers,
to my sigh of supplication.

Who could survive, Lord,
if You kept count of every sin?

But forgiveness is Yours,
that we may worship You.

My whole being waits for the Lord,
with hope I wait for His word.

I yearn for the Lord
more eagerly than watchmen for the dawn, watchmen for the dawn.

Put your hope in the Lord,
for the Lord is generous with mercy.

Abundant is His power to redeem;
He will redeem the people Israel from all sin.

Psalm 130

Of all the commandments in existence today that structure a Jewish life, only three are directed primarily (and in one case, exclusively) to women. These are: *hallah* (removing a small portion of dough when baking bread and tossing it into the fire); *hadlakah* (lighting candles on Shabbat and holidays); and *niddah* or *tohorat hamishpahah* (the sexual abstinence and reunion surrounding a wife's monthly cycle).

Tradition assigns various reasons—not always complimentary—to explain why these three commandments were given to women. But seen at as a unit, in a more symbolic light, this triad offers a cherished, if partial, view of the woman as

provider for her family and, by extension, the Jewish community. She is provider of nourishment and sustenance (*hallah*); vision, wisdom, and learning (*hadlakah*); and love, companionship and regeneration (*tohorat hamishpahah*).

This book begins with the first of these three commandments. In the days of the Temple, the ritual of *hallah* was performed by the priests at the altar as part of their holy service to God. The sacrifice of a small portion of dough signified the Jewish people's recognition that everything they had, everything they grew, everything they made, was a gift from God.

How do you repay God for all His

Ogni Donna prima di levare la חלה dirà la seguente Orazione

שִׁיר הַמַּעֲלוֹת מִמַּעֲמַקִּים קְרָאתִיךָ יְיָ: אֲדֹנָי שִׁמְעָה בְקוֹלִי תִּהְיֶינָה אָזְנֶיךָ קַשֻּׁבוֹת לְקוֹל תַּחֲנוּנָי: אִם־עֲוֹנוֹת תִּשְׁמָר־יָהּ אֲדֹנָי מִי יַעֲמֹד: כִּי־עִמְּךָ הַסְּלִיחָה לְמַעַן תִּוָּרֵא: קִוִּיתִי יְיָ קִוְּתָה נַפְשִׁי וְלִדְבָרוֹ הוֹחָלְתִּי: נַפְשִׁי לַאדֹנָי מִשֹּׁמְרִים לַבֹּקֶר שֹׁמְרִים לַבֹּקֶר: יַחֵל יִשְׂרָאֵל אֶל־יְיָ כִּי־עִם־יְיָ הַחֶסֶד וְהַרְבֵּה עִמּוֹ פְדוּת: וְהוּא יִפְדֶּה אֶת־יִשְׂרָאֵל מִכֹּל עֲוֹנוֹתָיו:

kindness? What do you give to the One who not only has everything but gives everything? The fact is, you cannot really give anything. You can only return what you have received. That is what *hallah* is, giving back to God part of what He gives us. And that is why it is in the form of raw dough. To give grain back in its pure state is to fail to demonstrate our ability to use our God-given talents. To give back baked bread is to fail to recognize the difference between God's needs and human needs.

Significantly, the primary domain of this commandment, the sole sacrificial remnant of the Temple cult, is the woman's. The commandment of separating a portion of the dough, therefore, identifies the woman with the holy class of priests and transforms the home's humble hearth into the Temple's sacrificial altar.

Psalm 130 may have been placed here due to its theme and to a play on words.

The psalm begins by addressing God, reminding Him that humanity could not survive without divine forgiveness and that we, the petitioners, both as individuals and as the people Israel, rely on God to deal kindly with us. Asking forgiveness, petitioning God, giving thanks—such are the moods of sacrifice. *Hafrashat hallah,* as a remnant of the sacrifices, vivifies these themes of forgiveness and petition and thanks. Yet Psalm 130 is not

BLESSED are You, Lord our God, King of the Universe, who has sanctified us with His commandments and commanded us to separate the *hallah*.

MAY IT BE Your will that our dough be blessed through the work of our hands, just as blessings attended the handiwork of our mothers Sarah, Rebecca, Rachel, and Leah. May the words of Torah be true for us, as it is written: "The finest of your baking will you give to the priest, so that your houses may be blessed" (Ezekiel 44:30). Amen. So may it be Your will.

the only psalm to express these themes. Why then was it chosen? Perhaps because of a fortuitous phrase which aurally unites ancient psalm with modern *mitzvah*; the root _____ (to wait expectantly) is used twice here, creating a sound reminiscent of *hallah*, joining in one utterance text and deed, hope and commitment.

Typical of most holy books, this *siddur* begins on page 2, in an acknowledgment that no human effort can ever be complete; that perfection belongs only to God.

Feeding her family was a primary responsibility for the married woman. Here, the female head of the household calls upon God to bless the work of her hands, even as the efforts of her ancestors Sarah, Rebecca, Rachel, and Leah were blessed. The matriarchs are invoked many times throughout this prayer book as models, not for the way they acted toward God, but for the way God acted toward them. The petitioner uses them as reminders, as the measure, for the way God should respond to her.

Still, the ritual of *hallah* itself is humbling. *Hallah* is taken from the dough after much labor has fashioned it. A pinch, a toss, and the work is ashes. So it is sometimes with life's labor. *Hallah* teaches us the lessons of loss, failure, and ultimate success.

בָּרוּךְ אַתָּה יְיָ אֱלֹקֵינוּ מֶלֶךְ הָעוֹלָם אֲשֶׁר קִדְּשָׁנוּ בְּמִצְוֹתָיו וְצִוָּנוּ לְהַפְרִישׁ חַלָּה:

יְהִי רָצוֹן מִלְּפָנֶיךָ שֶׁתִּתְבָּרַךְ עִסָּתֵנוּ עַל יָדֵנוּ כְּמוֹ שֶׁשָּׁרְתָה בְּרָכָה עַל־יְדֵי שָׂרָה רִבְקָה רָחֵל וְלֵאָה אִמּוֹתֵינוּ וִיקֻיַּם בָּנוּ מִקְרָא שֶׁכָּתוּב וְרֵאשִׁית עֲרִיסוֹתֵיכֶם תִּתְּנוּ לַכֹּהֵן לְהָנִיחַ בְּרָכָה אֶל־בֵּיתֶךָ: אָמֵן כֵּן יְהִי רָצוֹן:

The verse from Ezekiel (44:30) is quoted to remind God of the divine promise to bless every home that keeps the commandment of *hallah*. This verse echoes Numbers 15:20–21, which provides an even closer connection to the commandment. Indeed, Numbers 15:20 explicitly mentions the word *hallah* (which Ezekiel does not), and Numbers 15:21 states that the commandment will endure for all generations. Why was the verse from Ezekiel preferred? No doubt because of its tender and explicit reference to a blessing on the home.

The standard blessing formula begins by addressing God as "You" but shifts midway and addresses God as "He." (The traditional male imaging of God found in the Hebrew has been maintained throughout this translation.) Some say the formula reflects the human effort to approach God and to achieve a degree of intimacy (second person), an effort that, due to the absolute otherness of God, ultimately must fail (third person). Others think it represents the stages of a true journey toward God: one's love of God creates a desire to draw close to God (hence "You"). But one's fear of God creates a desire for distance from God (hence "Him"). This common formula, therefore, is seen as reflecting our ambivalent approaches toward God.

OF DAVID. O Lᴏʀᴅ, I set my hope on You;
  my God, in You I trust;
  may I not be disappointed,
  may my enemies not exult over me.
O let none who look to You be disappointed;
  let the faithless be disappointed; empty.
Let me know Your paths, O Lᴏʀᴅ;
  teach me Your ways;
  guide me in Your true way and teach me,
  for You are God, my deliverer;
  it is You I look to at all times.
O Lᴏʀᴅ be mindful of Your compassion
  and Your faithfulness;
  they are old as time.
Be not mindful of my youthful sins and transgressions;
  in keeping with Your faithfulness consider what is in my
    favor,
  as befits Your goodness, O Lᴏʀᴅ.
Good and upright is the Lᴏʀᴅ;
  therefore He shows sinners the way.
He guides the lowly in the right path,
  and teaches the lowly His way.
All the Lᴏʀᴅ's paths are steadfast love
  for those who keep the decrees of His covenant.
As befits Your name, O Lᴏʀᴅ,
  pardon my iniquity though it be great.

(continued)

לְדָוִד אֵלֶיךָ יְיָ נַפְשִׁי אֶשָּׂא: אֱלֹקַי בְּךָ בָטַחְתִּי אַל־
אֵבוֹשָׁה אַל־יַעַלְצוּ אוֹיְבַי לִי: גַּם כָּל־קֹוֶיךָ לֹא יֵבֹשׁוּ
יֵבֹשׁוּ הַבּוֹגְדִים רֵיקָם: דְּרָכֶיךָ יְיָ הוֹדִיעֵנִי אֹרְחוֹתֶיךָ
לַמְּדֵנִי: הַדְרִיכֵנִי בַאֲמִתֶּךָ | וְלַמְּדֵנִי כִּי־אַתָּה אֱלֹקֵי
יִשְׁעִי אוֹתְךָ קִוִּיתִי כָּל־הַיּוֹם: זְכָר־רַחֲמֶיךָ יְיָ וַחֲסָדֶיךָ כִּי
מֵעוֹלָם הֵמָּה: חַטֹּאות נְעוּרַי | וּפְשָׁעַי אַל־תִּזְכֹּר
כְּחַסְדְּךָ זְכָר־לִי־אַתָּה לְמַעַן טוּבְךָ יְיָ: טוֹב־וְיָשָׁר יְיָ
עַל־כֵּן יוֹרֶה חַטָּאִים בַּדָּרֶךְ: יַדְרֵךְ עֲנָוִים בַּמִּשְׁפָּט
וִילַמֵּד עֲנָוִים דַּרְכּוֹ: כָּל־אָרְחוֹת יְיָ חֶסֶד וֶאֱמֶת לְנֹצְרֵי
בְרִיתוֹ וְעֵדֹתָיו: לְמַעַן שִׁמְךָ יְיָ וְסָלַחְתָּ לַעֲוֹנִי כִּי רַב־
הוּא:

(continued)

Whoever fears the LORD,
    he shall be shown what path to choose.
He shall live a happy life,
    and his children shall inherit the land.
The counsel of the LORD is for those who fear Him;
    to them He makes known His covenant.
My eyes are ever toward the LORD,
    for He will loose my feet from the net.

Turn to me, have mercy on me,
    for I am alone and afflicted.
My deep distress increases;
    deliver me from my straits.
Look at my affliction and suffering,
    and forgive all my sins.
See how numerous my enemies are,
    and how unjustly they hate me!

Protect me and save me;
    let me not be disappointed,
    for I have sought refuge in You.
May integrity and uprightness watch over me,
    for I look to You.
O God, redeem Israel
    from all its distress.

Psalm 25

Psalm 25 echoes the key words of Psalm 130. Themes of forgiveness, expectations, and redemption swirl throughout. Both psalms end by calling upon God to redeem the people Israel, but the two final requests differ substantively. Psalm 130 calls for Israel's redemption (or forgiveness) from sin, while Psalm 25 calls for Israel's redemption (or protection) from oppression.

As a unit, Psalms 25 and 34 (both alphabetic acrostics in the Hebrew, where the initial letters of all the verses are in alphabetical order) take the petitioner from a mood of need, request, and expectation, to one of fulfillment and joy.

Psalm 25 speaks to God, reminding Him of humanity's abiding trust, of the psalmist's expectation that if we are faithful, we will be rewarded, and if we slip and sin, we will be forgiven and shown the right way. Either way, due to God's mercy, our lives are full. On the other

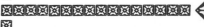

מִי־זֶה הָאִישׁ יְרֵא יְיָ יוֹרֶנּוּ בְּדֶרֶךְ יִבְחָר: נַפְשׁוֹ
בְּטוֹב תָּלִין וְזַרְעוֹ יִירַשׁ אָרֶץ: סוֹד יְיָ לִירֵאָיו וּבְרִיתוֹ
לְהוֹדִיעָם: עֵינַי תָּמִיד אֶל־יְיָ כִּי הוּא יוֹצִיא מֵרֶשֶׁת
רַגְלָי: פְּנֵה אֵלַי וְחָנֵּנִי כִּי יָחִיד וְעָנִי אָנִי: צָרוֹת לְבָבִי
הִרְחִיבוּ מִמְּצוּקוֹתַי הוֹצִיאֵנִי: רְאֵה עָנְיִי וַעֲמָלִי וְשָׂא
לְכָל־חַטֹּאותָי: רְאֵה אֹיְבַי כִּי רָבּוּ וְשִׂנְאַת חָמָס
שְׂנֵאוּנִי: שָׁמְרָה נַפְשִׁי וְהַצִּילֵנִי אַל־אֵבוֹשׁ כִּי חָסִיתִי
בָךְ: תֹּם וָיֹשֶׁר יִצְּרוּנִי כִּי קִוִּיתִיךָ: פְּדֵה אֱלֹקִים אֶת־
יִשְׂרָאֵל מִכֹּל צָרוֹתָיו:

hand, those who are without faith will live empty lives (verse 3). They will have nothing and produce nothing. Their work is nought but vanity.

The mood of Psalm 34, on the other hand, is one of received redemption. It is a psalm of exultation not addressed to God, but addressed to a human audience, a psalm by one intoxicated with God's goodness and eager to spread the message. The petitioner, wanting to share this knowledge of God, invites the audience (and the reader) to "taste and see how good the Lord is" (verse 9). *Hallah* (bread), the fulfillment of all need, is not the booty of the strong (lions have been reduced to starvation), but a gift to those who use speech wisely (verse 14). If the tongue is used for good and not evil, so it will be blessed for good and not evil.

In other words, what comes out of the mouth determines what will go in.

OF DAVID, when he feigned madness in the presence of
Abimelech, who turned him out, and he left.
I bless the LORD at all times;
  praise of Him is ever in my mouth.
I glory in the LORD;
  let the lowly hear it and rejoice.
Exalt the LORD with me;
  let us extol His name together.
I turned to the LORD, and He answered me;
  He saved me from all my terrors.
People look to Him and are radiant;
  let their faces not be downcast.
Here was a lowly man who called,
    and the LORD listened,
    and delivered him from all his troubles.
The angel of the LORD camps around those who fear Him
    and rescues them.
Taste and see how good the LORD is;
  happy the man who takes refuge in Him!
Fear the LORD, you His consecrated ones,
  for those who fear Him lack nothing.
Lions have been reduced to starvation.
  but those who turn to the LORD shall not lack any good.
Come, my sons, listen to me;
  I will teach you what it is to fear the LORD.
Who is the man who is eager for life,
  who desires years of good fortune?

(continued)

לְדָוִד בְּשַׁנּוֹתוֹ אֶת־טַעְמוֹ לִפְנֵי אֲבִימֶלֶךְ וַיְגָרֲשֵׁהוּ
וַיֵּלַךְ: אֲבָרֲכָה אֶת־יְיָ בְּכָל־עֵת תָּמִיד תְּהִלָּתוֹ בְּפִי: בַּיְיָ
תִּתְהַלֵּל נַפְשִׁי יִשְׁמְעוּ עֲנָוִים וְיִשְׂמָחוּ: גַּדְּלוּ לַיְיָ אִתִּי
וּנְרוֹמְמָה שְׁמוֹ יַחְדָּו: דָּרַשְׁתִּי אֶת־יְיָ וְעָנָנִי וּמִכָּל־
מְגוּרוֹתַי הִצִּילָנִי: הִבִּיטוּ אֵלָיו וְנָהָרוּ וּפְנֵיהֶם אַל־
יֶחְפָּרוּ: זֶה עָנִי קָרָא וַיְיָ שָׁמֵעַ וּמִכָּל־צָרוֹתָיו הוֹשִׁיעוֹ:
חֹנֶה מַלְאַךְ־יְיָ סָבִיב לִירֵאָיו וַיְחַלְּצֵם: טַעֲמוּ וּרְאוּ כִּי־
טוֹב יְיָ אַשְׁרֵי הַגֶּבֶר יֶחֱסֶה־בּוֹ: יְראוּ־אֶת־יְיָ קְדוֹשָׁיו
כִּי־אֵין מַחְסוֹר לִירֵאָיו: כְּפִירִים רָשׁוּ וְרָעֵבוּ וְדֹרְשֵׁי יְיָ
לֹא־יַחְסְרוּ כָל־טוֹב: לְכוּ בָנִים שִׁמְעוּ־לִי יִרְאַת יְיָ
אֲלַמֶּדְכֶם: מִי־הָאִישׁ הֶחָפֵץ חַיִּים אֹהֵב יָמִים לִרְאוֹת
טוֹב:

(continued)

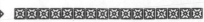

Guard your tongue from evil,
   your lips from deceitful speech.
Shun evil and do good,
   seek amity and pursue it.
The eyes of the LORD are on the righteous,
   His ears attentive to their cry.
The face of the LORD is set against evildoers,
   to erase their names from the earth.
They cry out, and the LORD hears,
   and saves them from all their troubles.
The LORD is close to the brokenhearted;
   those crushed in spirit He delivers
Though the misfortunes of the righteous be many
   the LORD will save him from them all.
Keeping all his bones intact,
   not one of them being broken.
One misfortune is the deathblow of the wicked;
   the foes of the righteous shall be ruined.
The LORD redeems the life of His servants;
   all who take refuge in Him shall not be ruined.

Psalm 34

Conclusion of the prayer said over hallah

נְצֹר לְשׁוֹנְךָ מֵרָע וּשְׂפָתֶיךָ מִדַּבֵּר מִרְמָה: סוּר
מֵרָע וַעֲשֵׂה־טוֹב בַּקֵּשׁ שָׁלוֹם וְרָדְפֵהוּ: עֵינֵי יְיָ אֶל־
צַדִּיקִים וְאָזְנָיו אֶל־שַׁוְעָתָם: פְּנֵי יְיָ בְּעֹשֵׂי רָע לְהַכְרִית
מֵאֶרֶץ זִכְרָם: צָעֲקוּ וַיְיָ שָׁמֵעַ וּמִכָּל־צָרוֹתָם הִצִּילָם:
קָרוֹב יְיָ לְנִשְׁבְּרֵי־לֵב וְאֶת־דַּכְּאֵי־רוּחַ יוֹשִׁיעַ: רַבּוֹת
רָעוֹת צַדִּיק וּמִכֻּלָּם יַצִּילֶנּוּ יְיָ: שֹׁמֵר כָּל־עַצְמוֹתָיו
אַחַת מֵהֵנָּה לֹא נִשְׁבָּרָה: תְּמוֹתֵת רָשָׁע רָעָה וְשֹׂנְאֵי
צַדִּיק יֶאְשָׁמוּ: פֹּדֶה יְיָ נֶפֶשׁ עֲבָדָיו וְלֹא יֶאְשְׁמוּ כָּל־
הַחוֹסִים בּוֹ:

Fine del Orazione della חלה

Prayers to Be Said
on Lighting the Shabbat Candles

Every woman, before lighting the Shabbat or holiday candles, says:

YOUR WORD is a lamp to my feet,
   a light for my path.
I have firmly sworn
   to keep Your just rules.
I am very much afflicted;
   O LORD, preserve me in accordance with Your word.
Accept, O LORD, my freewill offerings;
   teach me Your rules.
Though my life is always in danger,
   I do not neglect Your teaching.
Though the wicked have set a trap for me,
   I have not strayed from Your precepts.
Your decrees are my eternal heritage;
   they are my heart's delight.
I am resolved to follow Your laws
   to the utmost forever.

Psalm 119

The section on candlelighting opens with a selection from the grand Psalm 119. No doubt this section was chosen for its two opening verses, which speak both of a candle and a sworn dedication to uphold God's commandments. By placing this psalm here, the *siddur* transforms the

Ogni Donna prima di accendere il
lume di שבת , o di מועד , dirà

נֵר־לְרַגְלִי דְבָרֶךָ וְאוֹר לִנְתִיבָתִי: נִשְׁבַּעְתִּי וָאֲקַיֵּמָה
לִשְׁמֹר מִשְׁפְּטֵי צִדְקֶךָ: נַעֲנֵיתִי עַד־מְאֹד יְיָ חַיֵּנִי
כִדְבָרֶךָ: נִדְבוֹת פִּי רְצֵה־נָא יְיָ וּמִשְׁפָּטֶיךָ לַמְּדֵנִי:
נַפְשִׁי בְכַפִּי תָמִיד וְתוֹרָתְךָ לֹא שָׁכָחְתִּי: נָתְנוּ רְשָׁעִים
פַּח לִי וּמִפִּקּוּדֶיךָ לֹא תָעִיתִי: נָחַלְתִּי עֵדְוֹתֶיךָ לְעוֹלָם
כִּי־שְׂשׂוֹן לִבִּי הֵמָּה: נָטִיתִי לִבִּי לַעֲשׂוֹת חֻקֶּיךָ לְעוֹלָם
עֵקֶב:

ordinary glow of the candles into a halo of
divine light. By placing the psalm here,
the *siddur* makes each woman, each week,
a partner with God in the task of shed-
ding divine light upon all creation and of
spreading the divine word to all Israel.

15

MASTER of the Universe, even from Your exalted throne You can see that I attend to the task of lighting the candles of the holy Shabbat in order to fulfill and preserve the commandments of my Creator, in love and gladness of heart just as You have commanded me.

God does not want dutiful but vacuous, precise but cold, performance of rituals. Warmth and love, joy and gladness are as essential to the proper performance of the ritual as is calculated attendance to the detail.

Abiding by God's commandments, by definition, appears to be an act of obedience and not an act of volition. Yet in the twentieth century, to be willing to accept upon ourselves the *mitzvot* as binding

רִבּוֹן כָּל־הָעוֹלָמִים גָּלוּי וְיָדוּעַ לִפְנֵי כִּסֵּא כְבוֹדֶךְ
שֶׁאֲנִי בָּאתִי לְהַדְלִיק [dirà שבת di] נֵר שֶׁל שַׁבָּת קֹדֶשׁ
[dirà מועד di] נֵר שֶׁל יוֹם טוֹב מִקְרָא קֹדֶשׁ הַזֶּה
[dirà מועד e שבת di] נֵר שֶׁל שַׁבָּת קֹדֶשׁ וְשֶׁל יוֹם טוֹב מִקְרָא
קֹדֶשׁ הַזֶּה] לְקַיֵּם מִצְוַת בּוֹרְאִי בְּאַהֲבָה וּבְגִילָה
וּבְשִׂמְחַת לְבָבִי כַּאֲשֶׁר צִוִּיתָנִי:

commandments of God is to submit ourselves voluntarily to the commanding
nature of God's law. Such is the paradox
of faith entwined with modernity, freedom, and divine law.

This prayer in the original offers, par-
enthetically, all the permutations for how
it should be said, depending upon
whether the day is Shabbat, a holiday, or
both.

THEREFORE, Almighty, God of Israel, may it be Your desire to radiate light, joy, happiness, honor, goodness, mercy, prosperity, blessing, and peace upon those in the heavens and those here below; and bathe us, our souls, and our spirit in the light of Your luminous countenance. "For the radiance of a king's face grants life" (Proverbs 16:15). "For in You is the source of all life; by Your light do we see light" (Psalm 36:10). "Light is sown for the righteous" (Psalm 97:11). "The Lord is my light and my help" (Psalm 27:1). "The Lord is God, who sheds light upon us" (Psalm 118:27). "May the Lord be gracious to us and bless us. May He shine His countenance upon us. Selah" (Psalm 67:2). "May He shine His countenance upon us and be gracious to us" (adapted from Number 6:25), extending graciousness through the concealed light, the light of all life, about which it is written, "And the Lord said, 'Let there be light. And there was light'" (Genesis 1:3). Amen, Selah.

As she lights the candles for Shabbat or the holidays, she says:

BLESSED are You, Lord our God, King of the Universe, who sanctified us through His commandments and commanded us to kindle the light of [on Shabbat] the Holy Sabbath; [on a holiday] this holiday, a day of sacred assembly; [when Shabbat and a holiday coincide] the holy Sabbath and this holiday, a day of sacred assembly.

Disparate images of light tumble forward in a heap of verses reminding the petitioner of all the good we see in light. Light is blessing and guidance, security and life.

Reference to the concealed light recalls the popular rabbinic explanation of the

enigma of the creation of light: if the sun and the moon and the stars were created on the fourth day (Genesis 1:14–19), how could light be created on the first day (Genesis 1:3–5)? The primordial light, not bound by an orb, lit up the entire universe and enabled vision beyond the

יְהִי רָצוֹן מִלְפָנֶיךָ יְיָ אֱלֹקִים יְיָ אֱלֹקֵי יִשְׂרָאֵל שֶׁתַּשְׁפִּיעַ
אוֹרָה וְשִׂמְחָה וְשָׂשׂוֹן וִיקָר וְחֵן נָחֶסֶד וְרַחֲמִים וְרָצוֹן
וְחַיִּים טוֹבִים וּבְרָכָה וְשָׁלוֹם לָעֶלְיוֹנִים וְלַתַּחְתּוֹנִים
וְהָאִיר לָנוּ וּלְנַפְשׁוֹתֵינוּ וּלְרוּחֵנוּ וּלְנִשְׁמוֹתֵינוּ בְּאוֹר
פָּנֶיךָ הַמְּאִירִים כִּי בְאוֹר פְּנֵי מֶלֶךְ חַיִּים כִּי עִמְּךָ מְקוֹר
חַיִּים בְּאוֹרְךָ נִרְאֶה אוֹר. אוֹר זָרוּעַ לַצַּדִּיק, יְיָ אוֹרִי
וְיִשְׁעִי אֶל יְיָ וַיָּאֶר לָנוּ. אֱלֹקִים יְחָנֵּנוּ וִיבָרְכֵנוּ יָאֵר פָּנָיו
אִתָּנוּ סֶלָה. יָאֵר יְיָ פָּנָיו אֵלֵינוּ וִיחֻנֵּנוּ לְהָאוֹר הַגָּנוּז
לְאוֹר הַחַיִּים שֶׁעָלָיו נֶאֱמַר וַיֹּאמֶר אֱלֹקִים יְהִי אוֹר וַיְהִי
אוֹר: אָמֵן סֶלָה וָעֶד:

E qui accenderà il lume di שבת,
o מועד, dicendo.

בָּרוּךְ אַתָּה יְיָ אֱלֹקֵינוּ מֶלֶךְ הָעוֹלָם אֲשֶׁר קִדְּשָׁנוּ
בְּמִצְוֹתָיו וְצִוָּנוּ עַל הַדְלָקַת נֵר שֶׁל [dirà שבת di] שַׁבָּת
קֹדֶשׁ: [dirà מועד di] יוֹם טוֹב מִקְרָא קֹדֶשׁ הַזֶּה:
[dirà מועד e שבת di] שַׁבָּת קֹדֶשׁ וְשֶׁל יוֹם טוֹב מִקְרָא
קֹדֶשׁ הַזֶּה:

now-natural limits of sight. However, anticipating humanity's factious and arrogant behavior, God withdrew the fullness of the light, and hence the full power of sight, and created the limiting orbs in the sky. But the primordial light was not destroyed. It is being stored in God's special place of treasures, waiting for the end of time when it will once again illumine the world for the righteous (*Hagigah* 12a).

And then she says:

GOD OF ISRAEL, may it be Your will to be gracious to me and to my husband [and if she has children, add: and to my children] and to all my family and the people of Israel. Grant us long life and full health, security from all evil, prosperity in all good. Think well of us; bless us. Be mindful of our needs for care and mercy. Bless us with many blessings. Fill our household with everything that is good. Let Your holy presence dwell among us. May there not be counted among us a childless man or a barren woman, a widow or widower. May our children not die in our lifetime. May we be spared all suffering. Grant that I be worthy of giving life to knowing, wise, and distinguished children and grandchildren who love the Lord and who are God-fearing and God-struck. May they light up the world through their learning and kindness, doing the work of their Creator. Please, now hear my plea; for the sake of Sarah, Rebecca, Rachel, and Leah, our mothers. Let our candle shine forth. May it neither flicker nor ever be extinguished. Shine Your face upon us, so we will be saved, we and all Israel, speedily and in our day. Amen. Selah.

The prayers in the traditional *siddur* are mostly communal. The prayers in this *siddur* are mostly personal. The woman here petitions on her own behalf, and on behalf of her loved ones. But, since no Jew approaches God alone, the woman's personal prayer quickly enlarges to encompass requests for the well-being of all Israel. Personal good is embedded in the communal good. And the apparent hue poi dirà

יְהִי רָצוֹן מִלְּפָנֶיךָ יְיָ אֱלֹקִים אֱלֹקֵי יִשְׂרָאֵל שֶׁתְּחוֹנֵן לִי
וּלְאִישִׁי [se aura figli] (וּלְבָנַי) וּלְכָל־קְרוֹבַי וּלְכָל־
יִשְׂרָאֵל חַיִּים טוֹבִים וַאֲרֻכִּים בְּבְרִיאוּת שְׁלֵמָה בְּהַצָּלָה
מִכָּל־רָע, וּבְהַצְלָחָה בְּכָל־טוֹב, וְזָכְרֵנוּ בְּזְכִירָה טוֹבָה
וּבְרָכָה, וּפָקְדֵנוּ בִּפְקֻדַּת יְשׁוּעָה וְרַחֲמִים, וּתְבָרְכֵנוּ
בְּרָכוֹת גְּדוֹלוֹת, וְתַשְׁלִים בָּתֵּינוּ בְּטוֹבוֹת רַבּוֹת
עֲצוּמוֹת, וְשַׁכֵּן שְׁכִינָתְךָ בֵּינֵינוּ. וְלֹא יִהְיֶה בָּנוּ לֹא עָקָר
וְלֹא עֲקָרָה לֹא שָׁכוּל וְלֹא שְׁכוּלָה לֹא אַלְמוֹן וְלֹא
אַלְמָנָה וְלֹא יִהְיֶה בָּנוּ דְּבָרִים רָעִים כְּלָל, וְתִזַּכֵּנִי
לְהוֹלִיד בָּנִים וּבְנֵי בָנִים חֲכָמִים וּנְבוֹנִים וִידוּעִים אֹהֲבֵי
יְיָ יִרְאֵי אֱלֹקִים בַּיְיָ דְבֵקִים שֶׁיָּאִירוּ עוֹלָמִים בַּתּוֹרָה
וּבְמַעֲשִׂים טוֹבִים וּבְכָל־מְלֶאכֶת עֲבֹדַת הַבּוֹרֵא,
וּשְׁמַע־נָא אֶת־תְּחִנָּתִי בָּעֵת וּבָעוֹנָה הַזֹּאת בִּזְכוּת
שָׂרָה וְרִבְקָה רָחֵל וְלֵאָה אִמּוֹתֵינוּ וְהָאֵר נֵרֵנוּ שֶׁלֹּא
יִדְעַךְ וְלֹא יִכְבֶּה לְעוֹלָם וְהָאֵר פָּנֶיךָ וְנִוָּשֵׁעָה וּבְכָל־
עַמְּךָ יִשְׂרָאֵל בִּמְהֵרָה בְּיָמֵינוּ אָמֵן סֶלָה וָעֶד:

mility of the petitioner (apparent because any noncommanded approach to God assumes a dash of bravado) is bolstered by the righteous worthiness of the matriarchs.

The theme of conceiving and bearing children, only touched upon here, is paramount throughout the rest of this *siddur*.

21

AND HANNAH PRAYED:

My heart exults in the Lord;
I have triumphed through the Lord.
I gloat over my enemies;
I rejoice in Your deliverance.
There is no holy one like the Lord,
Truly, there is none beside You;
There is no rock like our God.
Talk no more with lofty pride,
Let no arrogance cross your lips!
For the Lord is an all-knowing God;
By Him actions are measured.
The bows of the mighty are broken,
And the faltering are girded with strength.
Men once sated must hire out for bread;
Men once hungry hunger no more.
While the barren woman bears seven,
The mother of many is forlorn.
The Lord deals death and gives life,
Casts down into Sheol and raises up.
The Lord makes poor and makes rich;
He casts down, He also lifts high.
He raises the poor from the dust,
Lifts up the needy from the dunghill,
Setting them with nobles,
Granting them seats of honor.

(continued)

This joyous prayer is one of the very few biblical passages ascribed to a woman. Recited by Hannah after the birth, indeed after the weaning, of her long-awaited son, Samuel, the prayer serves two purposes here. It reinforces the authenticity of women spontaneously offering personal prayers. It serves as an incantation, a sympathetic charm, as if to say: even as Hannah, who was once barren, was able to rejoice over the birth of a healthy child, so may I be blessed to rejoice over the birth of a healthy child. The prayer also provides an additional measure of merit, by enlisting the memory and piety of Hannah on behalf of the mother-to-be (just in case the invocation of the four matriarchs is not sufficient).

The rabbis saw in Hannah the model par excellence of private petitionary prayer. According to rabbinic tradition, not only did Hannah compose the victory

וַתִּתְפַּלֵּל חַנָּה וַתֹּאמַר עָלַץ לִבִּי בַּיְיָ רָמָה קַרְנִי בַּיְיָ רָחַב פִּי עַל־אוֹיְבַי כִּי שָׂמַחְתִּי בִּישׁוּעָתֶךָ: אֵין־קָדוֹשׁ כַּיְיָ כִּי־אֵין בִּלְתֶּךָ וְאֵין צוּר כֵּאלֹקֵינוּ: אַל־תַּרְבּוּ תְדַבְּרוּ גְּבֹהָה גְבֹהָה יֵצֵא עָתָק מִפִּיכֶם כִּי אֵל דֵּעוֹת יְיָ וְלוֹ נִתְכְּנוּ עֲלִלוֹת: קֶשֶׁת גִּבֹּרִים חַתִּים וְנִכְשָׁלִים אָזְרוּ חָיִל: שְׂבֵעִים בַּלֶּחֶם נִשְׂכָּרוּ וּרְעֵבִים חָדֵלּוּ עַד־עֲקָרָה יָלְדָה שִׁבְעָה וְרַבַּת בָּנִים אֻמְלָלָה: יְיָ מֵמִית וּמְחַיֶּה מוֹרִיד שְׁאוֹל וַיָּעַל: יְיָ מוֹרִישׁ וּמַעֲשִׁיר מַשְׁפִּיל אַף־מְרוֹמֵם: מֵקִים מֵעָפָר דָּל מֵאַשְׁפֹּת יָרִים אֶבְיוֹן לְהוֹשִׁיב עִם־נְדִיבִים וְכִסֵּא כָבוֹד יַנְחִלֵם כִּי לַיְיָ מְצֻקֵי אֶרֶץ וַיָּשֶׁת עֲלֵיהֶם תֵּבֵל:

(continued)

song recorded here, but she also earlier composed the following prayer when at Shiloh and desperate for a child, she challenged God. In this prayer she offers not so much a petition, but an irrefutable line of argument. She reminds God of *His* scheme and *His* rules, the logic and justice of which demand she be given a child.

"Master of the Universe, of all the parts of woman that You created, not one was created in vain. Her eyes You made for seeing; her ears for hearing; her nose for smelling; her mouth for speaking; her hands for working; her legs for walking; her breasts for nursing. But these breasts which You gave to me, God, why do I not nurse from them? Give me a child, so I might nurse" (*Berakhot* 31b).

23

For the pillars of the earth are the LORD's;
He has set the world upon them.
He guards the steps of His faithful,
But the wicked perish in darkness—
For not by strength shall man prevail.
The foes of the LORD shall be shattered;
He will thunder against them in the heavens.
The LORD will judge the ends of the earth.
He will give power to His king.
And triumph to His anointed one.

I Samuel 2:1–10

OF DAVID The LORD is my light and my help;
   whom should I fear?
The LORD is the stronghold of my life,
   whom should I dread?
When evil men assail me
   to devour my flesh—
   it is they, my foes and my enemies,
   who stumble and fall.
Should an army besiege me,
   my heart would have no fear;
   should war beset me,
   still would I be confident.

(continued)

Chosen for the opening reference to God and "My light," this psalm has additional features that make it appropriate for the occasion of candlelighting. The reference to the "house of the Lord" in such a home-bound context allows, indeed encourages, an identity between God's holy Temple and the woman's domestic domain. Since God's house is long destroyed and we can no longer dwell there, then at least God can come and dwell in ours.

In Psalm 27, God is portrayed not only as light but as parent, providing protection from a harsh world. Human parents may falter, but God's shelter is everlasting.

רַגְלֵי חֲסִידָיו יִשְׁמֹר וּרְשָׁעִים בַּחֹשֶׁךְ יִדָּמּוּ כִּי־לֹא בְכֹחַ
יִגְבַּר־אִישׁ: יְיָ יֵחַתּוּ מְרִיבָיו עָלָיו בַּשָּׁמַיִם יַרְעֵם יְיָ
יָדִין אַפְסֵי־אָרֶץ וְיִתֶּן־עֹז לְמַלְכּוֹ, וְיָרֵם קֶרֶן מְשִׁיחוֹ:

לְדָוִד יְיָ ׀ אוֹרִי וְיִשְׁעִי מִמִּי אִירָא יְיָ מָעוֹז־חַיַּי מִמִּי
אֶפְחָד: בִּקְרֹב עָלַי ׀ מְרֵעִים לֶאֱכֹל אֶת־בְּשָׂרִי צָרַי
וְאֹיְבַי לִי הֵמָּה כָשְׁלוּ וְנָפָלוּ: אִם־תַּחֲנֶה עָלַי ׀ מַחֲנֶה
לֹא־יִירָא לִבִּי אִם־תָּקוּם עָלַי מִלְחָמָה בְּזֹאת אֲנִי
בוֹטֵחַ: אַחַת ׀ שָׁאַלְתִּי מֵאֵת־יְיָ אוֹתָהּ אֲבַקֵּשׁ שִׁבְתִּי
בְּבֵית־יְיָ כָּל־יְמֵי חַיַּי לַחֲזוֹת בְּנֹעַם־יְיָ וּלְבַקֵּר בְּהֵיכָלוֹ:

(continued)

"Though my father and mother abandon me . . ." In such a context, the
image of parents abandoning their children can be seen as encompassing not
only the petitioner as child, but the
petitioner as mother. No doubt she cannot imagine herself ever abandoning her
children. No doubt we all want to believe
that, like God, we will never abandon
our children. And yet, although God
exists forever, we do not. Read in this
context, this verse and the one preceding
it attempt to reassure the parents that
although they die, their child will never
be abandoned; for if one is deserving,
God's presence is steadfast.

One thing I ask of the LORD,
   only that do I seek:
   to live in the house of the LORD
   all the days of my life,
   to gaze upon the beauty of the LORD,
   to frequent His temple.
He will shelter me in His pavilion
   on an evil day,
   grant me the protection of His tent,
   raise me high upon a rock.
Now is my head high
   over my enemies roundabout;
   I sacrifice in His tent with shouts of joy,
   singing and chanting a hymn to the LORD.
Hear, O LORD, when I cry aloud;
   have mercy on me, answer me.
In Your behalf my heart says:
   "Seek My face!"
O LORD, I seek Your face.
Do not hide Your face from me;
   do not thrust aside Your servant in anger;
   You have ever been my help.
Do not forsake me, do not abandon me,
   O God, my deliverer.
Though my father and mother abandon me,
   the LORD will take me in.
Show me Your way, O LORD,
   and lead me on a level path
   because of my watchful foes.
Do not subject me to the will of my foes,
   for false witnesses and unjust accusers
   have appeared against me.
Had I not the assurance
   that I would enjoy the goodness of the LORD
   in the land of the living . . .
Look to the LORD;
   be strong and of good courage!
O look to the LORD!

Psalm 27

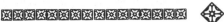

כִּי יִצְפְּנֵנִי ן בְּסֻכֹּה בְּיוֹם רָעָה יַסְתִּרֵנִי בְּסֵתֶר אָהֳלוֹ
בְּצוּר יְרוֹמְמֵנִי: וְעַתָּה יָרוּם רֹאשִׁי עַל־אֹיְבַי סְבִיבוֹתַי
וְאֶזְבְּחָה בְאָהֳלוֹ זִבְחֵי תְרוּעָה אָשִׁירָה וַאֲזַמְּרָה לַיְיָ:
שְׁמַע־יְיָ קוֹלִי אֶקְרָא וְחָנֵּנִי וַעֲנֵנִי: לְךָ ן אָמַר לִבִּי בַּקְּשׁוּ
פָנָי אֶת־פָּנֶיךָ יְיָ אֲבַקֵּשׁ: אַל־תַּסְתֵּר פָּנֶיךָ ן מִמֶּנִּי
אַל־תַּט בְּאַף עַבְדֶּךָ עֶזְרָתִי הָיִיתָ אַל־תִּטְּשֵׁנִי וְאַל־
תַּעַזְבֵנִי אֱלֹקֵי יִשְׁעִי: כִּי־אָבִי וְאִמִּי עֲזָבוּנִי וַיְיָ יַאַסְפֵנִי:
הוֹרֵנִי יְיָ דַּרְכֶּךָ וּנְחֵנִי בְּאֹרַח מִישׁוֹר לְמַעַן שׁוֹרְרָי: אַל־
תִּתְּנֵנִי בְּנֶפֶשׁ צָרָי כִּי קָמוּ־בִי עֵדֵי־שֶׁקֶר וִיפֵחַ חָמָס:
לוּלֵא הֶאֱמַנְתִּי לִרְאוֹת בְּטוּב יְיָ בְּאֶרֶץ חַיִּים: קַוֵּה
אֶל־יְיָ חֲזַק וְיַאֲמֵץ לִבֶּךָ וְקַוֵּה אֶל־יְיָ:

HALLELUJAH.

I praise the LORD with all my heart
  in the assembled congregation of the upright.
The works of the LORD are great,
  within reach of all who desire them.
His deeds are splendid and glorious;
   His beneficence is everlasting;
   He has won renown for His wonders.
The LORD is gracious and compassionate;
   He gives food to those who fear Him;
   He is ever mindful of His covenant.
He revealed to His people His powerful works,
  in giving them the heritage of nations.
His handiwork is truth and justice;
   all His precepts are enduring,
   well-founded for all eternity,
   wrought of truth and equity.
He sent redemption to His people;
   He ordained His covenant for all time;
   His name is holy and awesome.
The beginning of wisdom is the fear of the LORD;
  all who practice it gain sound understanding.
Praise of Him is everlasting.

Psalm 111

הַלְלוּיָהּ אוֹדֶה יְיָ בְּכָל־לֵבָב בְּסוֹד יְשָׁרִים וְעֵדָה: גְּדוֹלִים מַעֲשֵׂי יְיָ דְּרוּשִׁים לְכָל־חֶפְצֵיהֶם: הוֹד־וְהָדָר פָּעֳלוֹ וְצִדְקָתוֹ עֹמֶדֶת לָעַד: זֵכֶר עָשָׂה לְנִפְלְאוֹתָיו חַנּוּן וְרַחוּם יְיָ: טֶרֶף נָתַן לִירֵאָיו יִזְכֹּר לְעוֹלָם בְּרִיתוֹ: כֹּחַ מַעֲשָׂיו הִגִּיד לְעַמּוֹ לָתֵת לָהֶם נַחֲלַת גּוֹיִם: מַעֲשֵׂי יָדָיו אֱמֶת וּמִשְׁפָּט נֶאֱמָנִים כָּל־פִּקּוּדָיו: סְמוּכִים לָעַד לְעוֹלָם עֲשׂוּיִם בֶּאֱמֶת וְיָשָׁר: פְּדוּת שָׁלַח לְעַמּוֹ צִוָּה לְעוֹלָם בְּרִיתוֹ קָדוֹשׁ וְנוֹרָא שְׁמוֹ: רֵאשִׁית חָכְמָה יִרְאַת יְיָ שֵׂכֶל טוֹב לְכָל־עֹשֵׂיהֶם תְּהִלָּתוֹ עֹמֶדֶת לָעַד:

HALLELUJAH.

Happy is the man who fears the LORD,
  who is ardently devoted to His commandments.
His descendants will be mighty in the land,
  a blessed generation of upright men.
Wealth and riches are in his house,
  and his beneficence lasts forever.
A light shines for the upright in the darkness;
  he is gracious, compassionate, and beneficent.
All goes well with the man who lends generously,
  who conducts his affairs with equity.
He shall never be shaken;
  the beneficent man will be remembered forever.
He is not afraid of evil tidings;
  his heart is firm, he trusts in the LORD.
His heart is resolute, he is unafraid;
  in the end he will see the fall of his foes.
He gives freely to the poor;
  his beneficence lasts forever;
  his horn is exalted in honor.
The wicked man shall see it and be vexed;
  he shall gnash his teeth; his courage shall fail.
The desire of the wicked shall come to nothing.

Psalm 112

Psalms 111 and 112 share a unique structural form: written in an alphabetic acrostic, both the beginning and middle of each verse contribute a letter to the completion of the *alef bet*. According to Rashi, these psalms together form a complementary couplet, the first singing the splendor of God, the second telling of the merits of the righteous on earth (Psalm 111:4).

Tradition reads in the word *zekher* (renown), a reminder of the observance of Shabbat ("*Zakhor*," "Remember the Sabbath day and keep it holy"), as well as of all the *mitzvot* ("*Uzakhartem*," "You shall remember all the Lord's com-

הַלְלוּיָהּ ׀ אַשְׁרֵי־אִישׁ יָרֵא אֶת־יְיָ בְּמִצְוֹתָיו חָפֵץ
מְאֹד: גִּבּוֹר בָּאָרֶץ יִהְיֶה זַרְעוֹ דּוֹר יְשָׁרִים יְבֹרָךְ: הוֹן־
וָעֹשֶׁר בְּבֵיתוֹ וְצִדְקָתוֹ עֹמֶדֶת לָעַד: זָרַח בַּחֹשֶׁךְ אוֹר
לַיְשָׁרִים חַנּוּן וְרַחוּם וְצַדִּיק: טוֹב־אִישׁ חוֹנֵן וּמַלְוֶה
יְכַלְכֵּל דְּבָרָיו בְּמִשְׁפָּט: כִּי־לְעוֹלָם לֹא־יִמּוֹט לְזֵכֶר
עוֹלָם יִהְיֶה צַדִּיק: מִשְּׁמוּעָה רָעָה לֹא יִירָא נָכוֹן לִבּוֹ
בָּטֻחַ בַּיְיָ: סָמוּךְ לִבּוֹ לֹא יִירָא עַד אֲשֶׁר־יִרְאֶה בְצָרָיו:
פִּזַּר ׀ נָתַן לָאֶבְיוֹנִים צִדְקָתוֹ עֹמֶדֶת לָעַד קַרְנוֹ תָּרוּם
בְּכָבוֹד: רָשָׁע יִרְאֶה ׀ וְכָעָס שִׁנָּיו יַחֲרֹק וְנָמָס תַּאֲוַת
רְשָׁעִים תֹּאבֵד:

---

mandments") (Numbers 15:39).

Teref (Psalm 111:5), to some, is simply food. To others, it is an allusion to the manna that miraculously fed the Jews in the desert. And it is because a double portion of manna was to be gathered in preparation for Shabbat that we begin our Shabbat meals with two *hallot*, and a double appreciation of God's beneficence.

Verse 4 of Psalm 112, although difficult to understand, speaks of a bright light that pierces the darkness for the righteous. Recited within the context of candlelighting, it is as if each week, each woman, as God's chosen partner, assumes the task of kindling this numinous light.

MY GOD and God of my forebears, may it be Your desire, for the sake of Your exalted name—richly bedecked with the crowns of faithfulness—to command Your angels, the appointed guardians of human endeavors, to protect me and my husband [and if she has children, add: my children] and all Israel from dreadful accidents and lingering illness; from all fear and fright and worry and panic and trembling; from evil spirits and demons; from epileptic fits, diphtheria, and depression; from any change in the wind, from all plague and epidemic; from all dread, all nightmares, and all witchcraft. May we win the affection of both God and our neighbors. Give us worthy sons so that we may raise them to study Your Torah, and help them to establish families of their own, and to bring goodness to the world. Let them not suffer from any weakness or illness or disease. Let them be strong in spirit and body so that they may learn and teach and observe and preserve all the words of the Torah, now and forever.

Throughout the ages, Jews believed that angels, both good and bad, populated the world around them, guiding their affairs. But angels were not free spirits; each performed an assigned task. In this prayer, the petitioner asks that God instruct the angels who oversee human affairs to protect her household and all Israel.

This prayer, like others in the book, asks for sons. Why? One traditional answer is based on the last words of the prayer: so that our sons will be able "to observe and preserve the entire substance of Your Torah." Women were exempt from positive (thou shall . . .), time-bound (prescribed by clock or calendar) commandments. Hence they could not

יְהִי רָצוֹן מִלְּפָנֶיךָ יְיָ אֱלֹקַי וֵאלֹקֵי אֲבוֹתַי לְמַעַן שִׁמְךָ
הַגָּדוֹל הַמְכֻתָּר בְּכֶתֶר הָאֱמוּנָה שֶׁתְּצַוֶּה לְמַלְאָכֶיךָ
הַמְמֻנִּים עַל־עִסְקֵי בְּנֵי־אָדָם שֶׁיִּשְׁמְרוּ אוֹתִי וְאֶת
בַּעֲלִי [se avrà figli dirà] [וְאֶת בָּנַי] וְאֶת־כָּל־יִשְׂרָאֵל
מִכָּל־פְּגָעִים רָעִים וַחֲלָאִים רָעִים וְנֶאֱמָנִים וּמִכָּל־פַּחַד
וְאֵימָה וְיִרְאָה וְרַעַד וָרֶתֶת, וּמֵרוּחַ רָעָה וּמִשֵּׁדִין
וּמַלִּילִין וּמִכָּל חֳלִי הַנִּכְפֶּה וְאַסְכָּרָה וָחֳלִי מָרָה שְׁחוֹרָה
וּלְבָנָה וִירוּקָה וּמִכָּל־שִׁנּוּי אֲוִיר וּמִכָּל־דֶּבֶר וּמַגֵּפָה
וּמִכָּל־פַּחַד־לֵב וּמִכָּל־חֲלוֹמוֹת רָעִים וּמִכָּל־רוּחַ
וְכִשּׁוּף, וְנִהְיֶה נוֹשְׂאֵי־חֵן בְּעֵינֵי אֱלֹקִים וְאָדָם, וְתֶן לָנוּ
בָּנִים זְכָרִים כְּשֵׁרִים לְגַדְּלָם לְתַלְמוּד תּוֹרָה וּלְחֻפָּה
וּלְמַעֲשִׂים טוֹבִים, וְלֹא יִהְיֶה בָהֶם שׁוּם חַלָּשָׁה וְלֹא
רִפְיוֹן וְלֹא חֹלִי אֶלָּא יִהְיוּ חֲזָקִים בְּתֹקֶף לִלְמֹד וּלְלַמֵּד
לִשְׁמֹר וְלַעֲשׂוֹת וּלְקַיֵּם אֶת כָּל־דִּבְרֵי תַלְמוּד תּוֹרָתֶךָ
מֵעַתָּה וְעַד עוֹלָם:

observe, and therefore preserve, as many commandments as men.

Another suggestion is bound up with the mourner's *kaddish*. Until the twentieth century, only male relatives were permitted to recite the *kaddish* memorializing the dead. To fail to have a son meant to fail to have someone who could participate in the public ritual of reciting the *kaddish*.

Does this request for sons, and not daughters, reflect the woman's true feelings? Did all women pray for every pregnancy to yield a son? Were girls really less valued? Should we take these prayers at face value? The truth is, we just don't know. And the true answer may forever elude us.

And then she says the following verses three times:

THE LORD of hosts is with us. The God of Jacob is our stronghold (Psalm 46:12). LORD of hosts, happy is the one who trusts in You (Psalm 84:13). God save us. The King will answer us when we call (Psalm 20:20).

Then she says the following verse forward and backward three times:

YOU are my shelter,
You preserve me from distress;
You surround me with the joyous shout of deliverance.

Psalm 32:7

These three verses, recited as the last moments of the sixth day of the week give way to the holy Shabbat, also appear as a unit in late versions of the beautiful, succinct *Havdalah* service. This service is recited each Saturday night as the departing Shabbat Queen slips back across the threshold of holy time to be replaced by the hours of another weekday. Thresholds are places where one boundary gives way to another, where one domain yields to another. Thresholds are places where limits end, where gateways yawn, where lines blur. As such, they are vulnerable places. No wonder the image of God as a fortress, as a reliable and powerful ally, would be invoked at a time of unprotectedness. Together, these verses spin a triple thread of

E poi dirà tre volte tutti li
tre seguenti פסוקים .

יְיָ צְבָאוֹת עִמָּנוּ מִשְׂגָּב לָנוּ אֱלֹהֵי יַעֲקֹב סֶלָה: יְיָ
צְבָאוֹת אַשְׁרֵי אָדָם בֹּטֵחַ בָּךְ: יְיָ הוֹשִׁיעָה הַמֶּלֶךְ יַעֲנֵנוּ
בְיוֹם־קָרְאֵנוּ:

E poi dirà il seguente פסוק colle
annesse parole tre volte.

אַתָּה ׀ סֵתֶר לִי מִצַּר תִּצְּרֵנִי רָנֵּי פַלֵּט תְּסוֹבְבֵנִי סֶלָה:
סֶלָה תְּסוֹבְבֵנִי פַלֵּט רָנֵּי תִּצְּרֵנִי מִצַּר לִי סֵתֶר אַתָּה:

trust in God, a thread that, when combined
with the following verse, weaves a web of
divine might around the petitioners, offering protection and reassurance.

A bit of belief in magic and superstition
pervaded the medieval world, both Jewish
and non-Jewish. In this *siddur,* the words of
the *Tanakh*—the Bible—hold not only special meaning, but special powers, if recited
properly. Repetition by three breaks the
bonds of meaning, transforms words into
sounds, sounds into incantations, incantations into power. Psalm 32:7, in particular,
is full of rich sibilant and liquid sounds.
Not only do they speak of God's protective
shield, they weave it.

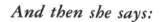

And then she says:

IN THE NAME of the Lord of Israel, *Shaddai Yah. Ehyeh* will be my stronghold and I will be strengthened by the name *Shaddai*. He will be my support. God, hear me. Be gracious to me and answer me. Be my help, God of Abraham, *Etan HaEzrahi;* God of Isaac, who was bound atop the altar; and God of Jacob, the innocent whom you saved from Esau and Laban. Permit me and my husband to merit sons so that they may occupy themselves with Torah and constantly seek Your company. May we raise them at the knees of great scholars, so that we may fulfill the words of the Torah: "Teach the laws to your children, speak often of them" (Deuteronomy 11:19). "Explain them to your children and your children's children" (Deuteronomy 4:9). May our children not die in our lifetime. May we never see them sad, but always joyful and happy. Give us long life, years of love and tenderness and peace, so that we may love You and revere You. Protect us from all evil and from all spirits and goblins and demons. Amen. So may it be Your will.

The conclusion of the prayers for lighting the candles

Having previously invoked the memories of Sarah, Rebecca, Rachel, Leah, and Hannah, the petitioner now reminds God of the faithful patriarchs Abraham, Isaac, and Jacob, and of a special moment of vulnerability when God interceded to protect each of them. The message is clear: just as You helped my ancestors, God, long ago, so should You now help me.

e poi dirà

בְּשֵׁם יְיָ אֱלֹקֵי יִשְׂרָאֵל שַׁדַּי יָהּ אֶהְיֶה יְהֶיֶה לִי בְּעֶזְרִי
וַאֲנִי אֶתְחַזֵּק בְּשֵׁם שַׁדַּי וְהוּא יִהְיֶה בְּסַעֲדִי, שְׁמַעְ־יָהּ
בְּקוֹלִי וְחָנֵּנִי וַעֲנֵנִי וֶהֱיֵה עוֹזֵר לִי אֱלֹקֵי אַבְרָהָם אֵיתָן
הָאֶזְרָחִי וֵאלֹקֵי יִצְחָק הַנֶּעֱקַד עַל־גַּבֵּי הַמִּזְבֵּחַ וֵאלֹקֵי
יַעֲקֹב הַתָּם אֲשֶׁר הַצַּלְתוֹ מֵעֵשָׂו וּמִלָּבָן, כֵּן תִּזְכֶּה־לִי
וּלְבַעֲלִי בָּנִים זְכָרִים שֶׁיִּהְיוּ עֹסְקִים בַּתּוֹרָה וּמְבַקְשִׁים
אֶת־פָּנֶיךָ תָּמִיד, וּלְגַדְּלָם בֵּין בִּרְכֵּי תַּלְמִידֵי חֲכָמִים,
וְיִתְקַיֵּם בָּנוּ מִקְרָא שֶׁכָּתוּב וְלִמַּדְתֶּם אֹתָם אֶת־בְּנֵיכֶם
לְדַבֵּר בָּם, וְהוֹדַעְתָּם לְבָנֶיךָ וְלִבְנֵי בָנֶיךָ, וְשֶׁלֹּא יָמוּתוּ
בְחַיֵּינוּ וְלֹא נִרְאֶה בָּהֶם עֶצֶב לְעוֹלָם, אֶלָּא שִׂמְחָה
וְחֶדְוָה, וְתֶן לָנוּ חַיִּים אֲרוּכִים וּשְׁנוֹת חַיִּים בְּאַהֲבָה
וּבְאַחְוָה וּבְשָׁלוֹם לְאַהֲבָה אוֹתְךָ וּלְיִרְאָה אֶת־שְׁמֶךָ,
וְתִשְׁמְרֵנוּ מֵעֵין הָרָע וּמִשֵּׁדִין לֵילִין וּמַזִּיקִין, אָמֵן כֵּן
יְהִי רָצוֹן:

Fine della Orazione per la הדלקת הנר

Here again the request for sons appears, as well as the desire to be spared from harm and disease, and to be blessed with a life buffered by companionship, love, and contentment.

The rabbis consider *Etan HaEzrahi* an epithet for Abraham. Perhaps this particular appellation is recalled here for the play on the word *zrh* (shine).

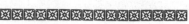

Prayers to Be Said on the Evening She Goes to Mikveh

Upon nightfall, on the evening when she goes to mikveh, she says:

A PSALM of David.

May the LORD answer you in time of trouble,
may the God of Jacob be your strength.
May He send you help from His sanctuary,
sustaining you from Zion.
May He remember all your offerings
and accept your sacrifices,
granting your heart's desires,
fulfilling all your hopes.

We shall sing of Your victory,
we shall acclaim the glory of our God.
May the Lord fulfill all that you ask.
Now I know that the LORD delivers His anointed.
He will answer from His heavenly abode,
bringing victory with mighty deeds.
Some trust in chariots, others in horses,
but we honor the name of the Lord our God.
They stumble and fall, but we rise and stand firm.
O LORD, deliver us! Answer us, O King, when we call.

Psalm 20

Jewish law requires that husbands and wives refrain from sexual pleasures during and immediately after the time of the woman's monthly cycle, the time when the woman is *niddah*. After the period of abstinence (according to tradition, minimally twelve days—at least five days for the flow plus seven "clean" days), the woman goes to the *mikveh*, a ritual bath, undresses completely, and fully immerses herself in the body of water. When she emerges from the waters of the *mikveh*, she emerges from her status as a *niddah*.

The ritual of the *mikveh* evokes a complex matrix of emotions. In part it is ennobling, for it heightens a woman's awareness of the cyclical nature of God's world and her role as partner in it. In part it is humbling, for the woman stands alone, naked before God, with no prayers

Ogni Donna, nella sera che dee andare al מקוה , subito che si fa notte dee dire.

לַמְנַצֵּחַ מִזְמוֹר לְדָוִד: יַעַנְךָ יְיָ בְּיוֹם צָרָה יְשַׂגֶּבְךָ שֵׁם ׀ אֱלֹהֵי יַעֲקֹב: יִשְׁלַח־עֶזְרְךָ מִקֹּדֶשׁ וּמִצִּיּוֹן יִסְעָדֶךָּ: יִזְכֹּר כָּל־מִנְחֹתֶיךָ וְעוֹלָתְךָ שַׁנֶּה סֶלָה: יִתֶּן־לְךָ כִלְבָבֶךָ וְכָל־עֲצָתְךָ יְמַלֵּא: נְרַנְּנָה ׀ בִּישׁוּעָתֶךָ וּבְשֵׁם־אֱלֹהֵינוּ נִדְגֹּל יְמַלֵּא יְיָ כָּל־מִשְׁאֲלוֹתֶיךָ: עַתָּה יָדַעְתִּי כִּי הוֹשִׁיעַ ׀ יְיָ מְשִׁיחוֹ יַעֲנֵהוּ מִשְּׁמֵי קָדְשׁוֹ בִּגְבוּרוֹת יֵשַׁע יְמִינוֹ: אֵלֶּה בָרֶכֶב וְאֵלֶּה בַסּוּסִים וַאֲנַחְנוּ בְּשֵׁם־יְיָ אֱלֹהֵינוּ נַזְכִּיר: הֵמָּה כָּרְעוּ וְנָפָלוּ וַאֲנַחְנוּ קַּמְנוּ וַנִּתְעוֹדָד: יְיָ הוֹשִׁיעָה הַמֶּלֶךְ יַעֲנֵנוּ בְיוֹם־קָרְאֵנוּ:

but her own, no gift but herself, no shield but her trust in the Lord. Most profoundly, the *mikveh* is a ritual enacting death and rebirth, feelings actualized by the descent into the gathered waters and the ascent afterward.

Mikveh is a ritual strangely both relational *and* personal. It is relational in that the result of the immersion affects not only the woman, but her husband as well.

Indeed, according to law, if her husband is away at the end of the twelve-day period, the woman needn't go to the *mikveh* until he returns. Yet, the performance of *mikveh* is starkly personal and individual; it is a pure, unguarded moment between woman and God.

She then says the following verses:

HAPPY is the one who has not followed the counsel of the wicked, or taken the path of sinners, or joined the company of the insolent (Psalm 1:1). I raise my eyes to the mountains. From where will my help come? (Psalm 121:1). A psalm of David: the Lord is my shepherd; I lack nothing (Psalm 23:1). May God be gracious to us and bless us; may He show us favor, Selah (Psalm 67:2). Hallelujah. Praise the Lord from the Heavens; praise Him on high (Psalm 148:1). O Lord, do not punish me in anger; do not chastise me in fury (Psalm 6:2). For the leaders, a psalm of David, when Nathan the prophet came to him after he had come to Bathsheba (Psalm 51:2). Praise the Lord, call on His name, proclaim His deeds among the peoples (Psalm 105:1). Sing forth, O you righteous, to the Lord; it is fit that the upright acclaim Him (Psalm 33:1).

This is a pastiche of opening verses from several psalms in the Book of Psalms, some of which appear in this *siddur*. Opening verses are notoriously introductory and do not lend themselves to being gently woven into an artful cloth. Such is the case here. Perhaps this disjointedness, this lack of a clear message reveals the underlying ambivalence toward sexual relations.

The articulated purpose of sexual relations, in Jewish tradition, is to conceive and bear children. That it might also be pleasurable is seen as potentially hazardous, diverting the couple's attention from the real desired end.

E poi dirà li seguenti פסוקים

אַשְׁרֵי הָאִישׁ אֲשֶׁר | לֹא הָלַךְ בַּעֲצַת רְשָׁעִים וּבְדֶרֶךְ
חַטָּאִים לֹא עָמָד וּבְמוֹשַׁב לֵצִים לֹא יָשָׁב: שִׁיר
לַמַּעֲלוֹת אֶשָּׂא עֵינַי אֶל־הֶהָרִים מֵאַיִן יָבֹא עֶזְרִי:
מִזְמוֹר לְדָוִד יְיָ רֹעִי לֹא אֶחְסָר: אֱלֹקִים יְחָנֵּנוּ וִיבָרְכֵנוּ
יָאֵר פָּנָיו אִתָּנוּ סֶלָה: הַלְלוּיָהּ | הַלְלוּ אֶת־יְיָ מִן־הַשָּׁמַיִם
הַלְלוּהוּ בַּמְּרוֹמִים: יְיָ אַל־בְּאַפְּךָ תוֹכִיחֵנִי וְאַל בַּחֲמָתְךָ
תְיַסְּרֵנִי: לַמְנַצֵּחַ מִזְמוֹר לְדָוִד: בְּבוֹא־אֵלָיו נָתָן הַנָּבִיא
כַּאֲשֶׁר־בָּא אֶל־בַּת־שָׁבַע: הוֹדוּ לַייָ קִרְאוּ בִשְׁמוֹ
הוֹדִיעוּ בָעַמִּים עֲלִילוֹתָיו: רַנְּנוּ צַדִּיקִים בַּייָ לַיְשָׁרִים
נָאוָה תְהִלָּה:

These verses jump back and forth from praising God to desiring His protection, from extolling the one who withstands temptation to asking God for understanding when we stumble. The emotions here slip from one feeling to another as quickly as they may in the act of love.

All this, the passion and the duty, the good and the sinful, the lust and the love, is invoked by recalling the names of David and Bathsheba. And we remember that David first saw Bathsheba as she was bathing, rededicating herself after her menstrual period.

 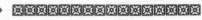

Afterward, she repeats the psalm, "May The Lord Answer You." Before leaving her house, she says the following prayer with profound devotion:

MAY IT BE Your will, my God and God of my forebears, God of Abraham, God of Isaac, and God of Jacob, that You be gracious to me so that on this night, which is now descending upon us in peace, my husband and I might conceive a child. Let the child created from this immersion be wise and truly God-fearing, unconditionally observant of Your laws, Your commandments, and Your judgments. Ruler of the Universe, please accept my plea and place in my womb a pure, unblemished soul. May I not be desecrated, God forbid, by a rebellious or undesirable son. Banish from me all impure thoughts and do not let the Evil Impulse seduce me, confounding me with wrongful imaginings. Make my husband's intentions pure when he desires to lie with me, so that we will merit bringing forth a child, pure and precious, of a good nature. May all my musings and my thoughts be for good so that I may be worthy of having all my requests fulfilled. For You are trustworthy and without equal. You accept the prayers of Your creatures. So may it be Your will. Amen. Do this for Your sake, for the sake of Your might and Your Torah and Your holiness. May the words of my mouth and the meditations of my heart be acceptable unto You, my Rock and my Redeemer.

The text now places the request for a child boldly on heaven's doorstep.

No longer a distant possibility, conception could happen this very night.

Placing this prayer here, so early in the evening, serves to channel all the evening's unfolding energies into the proper (and, God willing, successful) fulfillment

Replicherà poscia il מזמור di צרה ביום יי יענך.
Prima poi di uscire di casa, dirà con
grandissima כונה la seguente תפילה.

יְהִי רָצוֹן מִלְּפָנֶיךָ יְיָ אֱלֹקַי וֵאלֹקֵי וֵאלֹקֵי אֲבוֹתַי אֱלֹקֵי
אַבְרָהָם אֱלֹקֵי יִצְחָק וֵאלֹקֵי יַעֲקֹב שֶׁתְּחָנֵּנִי שֶׁאֶתְעַבֵּר
הַלַּיְלָה הַבָּאָה לִקְרָאתֵנוּ לְשָׁלוֹם מִבַּעֲלִי וְהַוָּלָד הַנּוֹצָר
מִטִּבִּילָה הַזֹּאת יִהְיֶה תַּלְמִיד חָכָם וִירֵא שָׁמַיִם בַּסֵּתֶר
וּמְקַיֵּם מִצְוֹתֶיךָ חֻקֶּיךָ וּמִשְׁפָּטֶיךָ לִשְׁמָם, רִבּוֹנוֹ שֶׁל
עוֹלָם קַבֵּל נָא אֶת תְּפִלָּתִי וְתַשְׁפִּיעַ בְּמֵעַי נְשָׁמָה זַכָּה
וּטְהוֹרָה וְלֹא אֶתְחַלֵּל חַס וְשָׁלוֹם בְּבָנִים שֶׁאֵינָם
הֲגוּנִים, וְהָסֵר מִמֶּנִּי כָּל־מַחֲשָׁבָה זָרָה וְתַצִּילֵנִי מִיֵּצֶר
הָרָע לְכָל יְסִיתֵנִי לְבַלְעֵנִי בְּמַחֲשָׁבוֹת רָעוֹת, וּלְבַעְלִי
תֵּן־בְּלִבּוֹ מַחֲשָׁבָה טוֹבָה כִּשְׁרוּצָה לְהִזְדַּוֵּג עִמִּי כְּדֵי
שֶׁנִּזְכֶּה לְהוֹלִיד בֵּן זָךְ וְטָהוֹר וְטוֹב לֵב וְיִהְיוּ כָּל
עֶשְׁתּוֹנוֹתַי וּמַחְשְׁבוֹתַי לְטוֹבָה כְּדֵי שֶׁאֶזְכֶּה שֶׁיִּמָּלְאוּ
מִשְׁאֲלוֹתַי, כִּי אֵל מֶלֶךְ יָחִיד וְנֶאֱמָן אַתָּה וּמְקַבֵּל
תְּפִלּוֹת יְצוּרֶיךָ, וְכֵן יְהִי רָצוֹן אָמֵן, עֲשֵׂה לְמַעַן שְׁמֶךָ,
עֲשֵׂה לְמַעַן יְמִינְךָ, עֲשֵׂה לְמַעַן תּוֹרָתֶךָ, עֲשֵׂה לְמַעַן
קְדֻשָּׁתֶךָ: יִהְיוּ לְרָצוֹן אִמְרֵי פִי וְהֶגְיוֹן לִבִּי לְפָנֶיךָ יְיָ
צוּרִי וְגוֹאֲלִי:

of the night's enterprise. And since it was
believed that the result of their deed is
influenced by their *kavannah* (that is, how
they approach the *mitzvah*) as well as by
its technical performance, the woman
prays that her heart and her husband's
desires be turned toward one another.

Upon leaving her house, she kisses the mezuzah *and recites the following verses:*

Guard me like the apple of Your eye;
  Hide me in the shadow of your wings (Psalm 17:8).
Hide me from a band of evil men, from a crowd of evil doers (Psalm 64:3).
He saved me from my fierce enemy, from foes too strong for me (Psalm 18:18).

E nell'uscire di casa baciando la מזוזה
dirà questi פסוקים .

שָׁמְרֵנִי כְּאִישׁוֹן בַּת־עָיִן וּבְצֵל כְּנָפֶיךָ תַּסְתִּירֵנִי:
תַּסְתִּירֵנִי מִסּוֹד מְרֵעִים מֵרִגְשַׁת פֹּעֲלֵי אָוֶן: יַצִּילֵנִי
מֵאֹיְבִי עָז וּמִשֹּׂנְאַי כִּי־אָמְצוּ מִמֶּנִּי:

And all the while she is walking, until she reaches the mikveh, *she repeats the following psalm.*

A SONG for ascents.
I turn my eyes to the mountains;
    from where will my help come?
My help comes from the LORD,
    maker of heaven and earth.
He will not let your foot give way;
    your guardian will not slumber;
See, the guardian of Israel
    neither slumbers nor sleeps!
The LORD is your guardian,
    the LORD is your protection
    at your right hand.
By day and the sun will not strike you,
    nor the moon by night.
The LORD will guard you from all harm;
    He will guard your life.
The LORD will guard your going and coming
    now and forever.

Psalm 121

Walking alone at night was frought with perils, both real and imagined. These selected verses on page 45 and the psalm that follows on page 47 ask for God's divine protection. Psalm 121 in particular speaks of God as our personal champion, forever our guardian through out all our life's journeys, day in and day out.

The poet juxtaposes the transcendent, majestic nature of God with the immanent, attentive nature of God. God is both distant Creator and immediate Protector. The moment the woman crosses her threshold, making herself vulnerable to the dangers of the night, she is reminded by the psalm that she can rely on God, the Almighty, the Ever-wakeful, to attend to her defense. Indeed, nature cannot harm her precisely because nature is subservient to God, its creator. And if God could create the heavens and the earth, and if God rules the heavenly

E tutto il tempo che va per istrada
sino che arrivi al Bagno, andrà
dicendo questo מזמור .

שִׁיר לַמַּעֲלוֹת אֶשָּׂא עֵינַי אֶל־הֶהָרִים מֵאַיִן יָבֹא עֶזְרִי:
עֶזְרִי מֵעִם יְיָ עֹשֵׂה שָׁמַיִם וָאָרֶץ: אַל־יִתֵּן לַמּוֹט רַגְלֶךָ
אַל־יָנוּם שֹׁמְרֶךָ: הִנֵּה לֹא־יָנוּם וְלֹא יִישָׁן שׁוֹמֵר
יִשְׂרָאֵל: יְיָ שֹׁמְרֶךָ יְיָ צִלְּךָ עַל־יַד יְמִינֶךָ: יוֹמָם הַשֶּׁמֶשׁ
לֹא־יַכֶּכָּה וְיָרֵחַ בַּלָּיְלָה: יְיָ יִשְׁמָרְךָ מִכָּל־רָע יִשְׁמֹר
אֶת־נַפְשֶׁךָ: יְיָ יִשְׁמָר־צֵאתְךָ וּבוֹאֶךָ מֵעַתָּה וְעַד־עוֹלָם:

---

lights, certainly God can give this woman
a child.

Married women visit the *mikveh* only at
night. Two reasons for this can be culled
from tradition. One is that the woman's
status as a *niddah* can be ended only after
the full count of days, a day, of course,
lasting from sunset to sunset. The earliest
moment a woman can immerse herself,
then, is after nightfall. Here, as with all
commandments, tradition anticipates an

eagerness to fulfill the *mitzvah* at the
earliest possible moment. This expectation, it seems, was translated into regu-
lation.

The second reason is one of modesty.
By visiting the *mikveh* after dark, the veil
of night hides the discreet comings and
goings of the modest, observant woman.

Just before she enters the mikveh, *while she is un-dressing, she says:*

MAY the favor of the LORD, our God, be upon us;
    let the work of our hands prosper,
    O prosper the work of our hands!
O you who dwell in the shelter of the Most High
    and abide in the protection of Shaddai—
I say of the LORD, my refuge and stronghold,
    my God in whom I trust,
    that He will save you from the fowler's trap,
    from the destructive plague.
He will cover you with His pinions;
    you will find refuge under His wings;
    His fidelity is an encircling shield.
You need not fear the terror by night,
    or the arrow that flies by day,
    the plague that stalks in the darkness,
    or the scourge that ravages at noon.
A thousand may fall at your left side,
    ten thousand at your right,
    but it shall not reach you.

(*continued*)

Psalm 91 (introduced by the last verse of Psalm 90, asking God to bless all that we do) is recited immediately before the petitioner immerses herself in the *mikveh*. It carries forward the theme of God's protective intervention. In a place not her own, the woman must undress, exposing herself to the dangers of the moment. But God will provide a protective shelter, God will take her under His wing. Divine protection, like the waters of the *mikveh*, surrounds and encompasses her. Even more, the psalm seems to promise that God, in tender consideration, will send His guardian angels to provide the petitioner a divine transport home.

The psalm anticipates a concern of the woman as she leaves the *mikveh* to return home. Emerging from the waters, the woman is now, more than at any other time of the month, spiritually and physically ready and available to her husband. She has spent hours preparing herself, purifying her soul and body for this reunion. Yet, purity invites vulnerability. The mood, the preparation, can be marred by the most minor intrusion or misstep. Her husband by right should be

Giunta poi che sia al Bagno,
nello spogliarsi dirà

וִיהִי ׀ נֹעַם אֲדֹנָי אֱלֹקֵינוּ עָלֵינוּ וּמַעֲשֵׂה יָדֵינוּ כּוֹנְנָה
עָלֵינוּ וּמַעֲשֵׂה יָדֵינוּ כּוֹנְנֵהוּ: יֹשֵׁב בְּסֵתֶר עֶלְיוֹן בְּצֵל
שַׁדַּי יִתְלוֹנָן: אֹמַר לַיְיָ מַחְסִי וּמְצוּדָתִי אֱלֹקַי אֶבְטַח־
בּוֹ: כִּי הוּא יַצִּילְךָ מִפַּח יָקוּשׁ מִדֶּבֶר הַוּוֹת: בְּאֶבְרָתוֹ ׀
יָסֶךְ לָךְ וְתַחַת־כְּנָפָיו תֶּחְסֶה צִנָּה וְסֹחֵרָה אֲמִתּוֹ: לֹא
תִירָא מִפַּחַד לָיְלָה מֵחֵץ יָעוּף יוֹמָם: מִדֶּבֶר בָּאֹפֶל
יַהֲלֹךְ מִקֶּטֶב יָשׁוּד צָהֳרָיִם: יִפֹּל מִצִּדְּךָ ׀ אֶלֶף וּרְבָבָה
מִימִינֶךָ אֵלֶיךָ לֹא יִגָּשׁ:

(continued)

the one who greets her first, the one who touches her first. On her way home, in her heightened state of readiness, even a chance brush on the leg by a dog can blemish, although not invalidate, her purification. Seen in this light, divine escort provides protection from the dangers of both injury and blemish.

The last three verses can be seen as referring to the child the woman hopes to conceive upon her return home. Because of the anticipated devotion of the child, God promises to offer blessings of security, honor, long life, salvation, and the constancy of His presence. What more could a mother want?

The words of the psalm also reflect the privacy of the acts of *mikveh* and sexual relations. The whole evening's activities are performed under a cloak of privacy. The words סתר and צל (verse 1) connote hiddenness while verse 4 speaks of being enfolded and wrapped within God's protective wings. Perhaps these words conjure up for the woman images of the tender moments to come.

You will see it with your eyes,
　　you will witness the punishment of the wicked.

Because you took the LORD—my refuge,
　　the Most High—as your haven,
　　no harm will befall you,
　　no disease touch your tent.
For He will order His angels
　　to guard you wherever you go.
They will carry you in their hands
　　lest you hurt your foot on a stone.
You will tread on cubs and vipers;
　　you will trample lions and asps.

"Because he is devoted to Me I will deliver him;
　　I will keep him safe, for he knows My name.
When he calls on Me, I will answer him;
　　I will be with him in distress;
　　I will rescue him and make him honored;
　　I will let him live to a ripe old age,
　　and show him My salvation."

Psalm 91

רַק בְּעֵינֶיךָ תַבִּיט וְשִׁלֻּמַת רְשָׁעִים תִּרְאֶה: כִּי־אַתָּה

יְיָ מַחְסִי עֶלְיוֹן שַׂמְתָּ מְעוֹנֶךָ: לֹא־תְאֻנֶּה אֵלֶיךָ

רָעָה וְנֶגַע לֹא־יִקְרַב בְּאָהֳלֶךָ: כִּי מַלְאָכָיו יְצַוֶּה

־לָּךְ לִשְׁמָרְךָ בְּכָל־דְּרָכֶיךָ: עַל־כַּפַּיִם יִשָּׂאוּנְךָ פֶּן

־תִּגֹּף בָּאֶבֶן רַגְלֶךָ: עַל־שַׁחַל וָפֶתֶן תִּדְרֹךְ תִּרְמֹס

כְּפִיר וְתַנִּין: כִּי בִי חָשַׁק וַאֲפַלְּטֵהוּ אֲשַׂגְּבֵהוּ כִּי־

יָדַע שְׁמִי: יִקְרָאֵנִי ׀ וְאֶעֱנֵהוּ עִמּוֹ־אָנֹכִי בְצָרָה אֲחַלְּצֵהוּ

וַאֲכַבְּדֵהוּ: אֹרֶךְ יָמִים אַשְׂבִּיעֵהוּ וְאַרְאֵהוּ בִּישׁוּעָתִי:

Then she immerses herself, saying this blessing:

BLESSED are You, Lord our God, Ruler of the Universe, Who sanctified us with His commandments and commanded us regarding ritual immersion.

While dressing, she again recites the psalm beginning, "I will raise my eyes to the mountains" (Psalm 121).

Upon arriving home, she kisses the mezuzah *and says the following psalm:*

A PSALM of David.
The Lord is my shepherd, I shall not want.
He allows me to lie down in green meadows.
He leads me beside the still waters to revive my spirit.
He guides me on the right path, for that is His nature.
Though I walk in the valley of the shadow of death,
I fear no harm, for You are with me.
Your staff and Your rod comfort me.
You prepare a banquet for me in the presence of my foes.
You anoint my head with oil; my cup overflows.
Surely goodness and kindness shall be my portion
All the days of my life.
And I shall dwell in the House of the LORD forever.

Psalm 23

Conclusion of the prayer for immersion

The common meaning of this popular psalm is remarkably transposed by its placement here, uttered upon the woman's return home to lie with her husband.

The allusion to lying down no longer simply means repose, but conjures up images of lying together; allusions to rest no longer simply mean refreshment but

Farà poscia la טבילה dicendo questa ברכה .

בָּרוּךְ אַתָּה יְיָ אֱלֹקֵינוּ מֶלֶךְ הָעוֹלָם אֲשֶׁר קִדְּשָׁנוּ בְּמִצְוֹתָיו וְצִוָּנוּ עַל הַטְּבִילָה:

Nello rivestirsi dirà di nuovo il מזמור di אשא עיני אל ההרים .

e giunta a casa baciando la מזוזה dira il seguente מזמור .

מִזְמוֹר לְדָוִד יְיָ רֹעִי לֹא אֶחְסָר: בִּנְאוֹת דֶּשֶׁא יַרְבִּיצֵנִי עַל־מֵי מְנֻחוֹת יְנַהֲלֵנִי: נַפְשִׁי יְשׁוֹבֵב יַנְחֵנִי בְמַעְגְּלֵי־צֶדֶק לְמַעַן שְׁמוֹ: גַּם כִּי־אֵלֵךְ בְּגֵיא צַלְמָוֶת לֹא־אִירָא רָע כִּי־אַתָּה עִמָּדִי שִׁבְטְךָ וּמִשְׁעַנְתֶּךָ הֵמָּה יְנַחֲמֻנִי: תַּעֲרֹךְ לְפָנַי ׀ שֻׁלְחָן נֶגֶד צֹרְרָי דִּשַּׁנְתָּ בַשֶּׁמֶן רֹאשִׁי כּוֹסִי רְוָיָה: אַךְ ׀ טוֹב וָחֶסֶד יִרְדְּפוּנִי כָּל־יְמֵי חַיָּי וְשַׁבְתִּי בְּבֵית־יְיָ לְאֹרֶךְ יָמִים:

Fine dell' Orazione per la טבילה

opportunities for re-creation. The last line, by coincidence of word and action, identifies the Lord's house with the petitioner's earthly abode. The one being addressed throughout the psalm is transformed into the petitioner's husband. The fullness of the psalm, seen in this light, reflects facets of sexual imagery.

Prayers to Be Said before Going to Bed with Her Husband

On the night of her immersion, before going to bed with her husband, the woman says the Shema *as usual, found in the back of the book, and then earnestly says the following prayer:*

EVERLASTING God, may it be Your desire to select for me a seed that is pure and holy so that it may tend to Your Work, be faithful to You, and pursue the study of Torah. May no harm come to me and may no force from the Other Side overpower me. Save me from a foreign god, from every evil enemy along my way, from the grasp of the decadent and lawless. For You are my hope. You are my surety And if, perchance, I become pregnant through my husband joining me tonight, it is because I sought to fulfill Your commandments. My soul rejoices in Your graciousness. Then I will sing to the Lord, for He has shown me kindness. Oh Lord, my God, please, show me graciousness and support me so that I might be truly worthy of raising this child, created to pursue Your holy tasks and to revere You wholeheartedly and sincerely guided by his loftiest desires. And may God forge this meditation into reality. Amen.

The Italian directions here offer a glimpse into the petitioner's daily prayer habits. The woman, it is assumed, recites the *Shema* upon going to bed every night. Tonight, however, she adds to her routine a prayer to be recited before uniting with her husband. She speaks to God once again of her desire to conceive a child.

In kabbalistic traditions, the *Sitra Ahra*, the Other Side, the domain of evil in this world, embodies the impulses for unholiness, a tempting, alluring, but evil diversion from the life of *mitzvot* and proper intent.

The phrase "Save me from the decadent and lawless, for You are my hope, You are my surety" is found with modest changes in

La sera della טבילה la donna, prima di andare
a letto consue Marito, dee dire il solito קריאת שמע
come si truova scritto nel fine di questo
libro, e poi dirà con grandissima כונה la seguente תפלה

יְהִי רָצוֹן מִלְּפָנֶיךָ צוּר הָעוֹלָמִים שֶׁתְּזַמֵּן לִי זֶרַע
טָהוֹר וְקָדוֹשׁ לַעֲבוֹדָתְךָ וּלְיִרְאָתְךָ וּלְתַלְמוּד תּוֹרָתֶךָ,
וְלֹא יִפְגַּע־בִּי שׁוּם פֶּגַע רָע וְלֹא שִׁלְטוֹן מִסִּטְרָא אַחֲרָא
וְתַצִּילֵנִי מִיַּד אֵל נֵכָר וּמִכָּל־אוֹיֵב רָע בַּדֶּרֶךְ וּמִכַּף
מָעֲוָל וְחוֹמֵץ, כִּי אַתָּה תִקְוָתִי וְאַתָּה אֱלֹקִים מִבְטָחִי
עָלֶיךָ, וְאִם בְּאוּלַי תַּעֲלֶה הֵרָיוֹנִי בְּהִתְלַוּוֹת אִישִׁי אֵלַי
הַלַּיְלָה הַזֶּה כִּי לַעֲשׂוֹת מִצְוֹתֶיךָ חָפַצְתִּי וְתָגֵל לִבִּי
בִּישׁוּעָתֶךָ אָשִׁירָה לַיְיָ כִּי־גָמַל עָלַי אַתָּה יְיָ אֱלֹקַי חָנֵּנִי
וַהֲקִימֵנִי עַד שֶׁאֶזְכֶּה לְגַדֵּל הַיֶּלֶד הַנּוֹצָר לַעֲבוֹדָתְךָ
וְיִרְאָתְךָ בֶּאֱמֶת וּבְלֵב שָׁלֵם כִּרְצוֹנוֹ הַטּוֹב וְהַיָּשָׁר,
וְכַוָּנָה טוֹבָה הַקָּדוֹשׁ בָּרוּךְ הוּא יְצָרְפֶנָּה לְמַעֲשֶׂה, אָמֵן.

Psalm 71. Of all the lines that speak of God's
beneficent protection, why was this chosen?
Perhaps because of the verse immediately following, which says, "From the womb of my
mother I have relied upon you. I sing Your
praises always." The mother-to-be suddenly
becomes the psalmist, singing praises of God's
steadfast protection. At the same time that we
look back to the months of mystery during
which the petitioner herself was created, we
look forward to the birth of the next generation, now forming in her womb, who will one
day sing their praises of God's steadfast protection.

FOR THE LEADER with instrumental music.
A psalm. A song.

May God be gracious to us and bless us;
    may He show us favor,
    that Your way be known on earth,
    Your deliverance among all nations.

Peoples will praise You, O God;
    all peoples will praise You.
Nations will exult and shout for joy,
    for You rule the peoples with equity,
    You guide the nations of the earth.
The peoples will praise You, O God;
    all peoples will praise You.

May the earth yield its produce;
    may God, our God, bless us.
May God bless us,
    and be revered to the ends of the earth.

Psalm 67

Conclusion

Much like the blessing formula, this psalm makes reference to God both in second and third person. Yet, unlike a blessing, this psalm begins in third person, shifts to second person, and moves back to third, as if the petitioner's respectful distance is overcome by the un- bridled impulse to draw closer to God, to grasp God's hand and to press into God's palm the words of her deepest desire. Protocol is recovered by the end of the psalm, and the petitioner retreats behind the language of third person.

In this psalm, the first person singular

לַמְנַצֵּחַ בִּנְגִינֹת מִזְמוֹר שִׁיר: אֱלֹהִים יְחָנֵּנוּ וִיבָרְכֵנוּ
יָאֵר פָּנָיו אִתָּנוּ סֶלָה: לָדַעַת בָּאָרֶץ דַּרְכֶּךָ בְּכָל־גּוֹיִם
יְשׁוּעָתֶךָ: יוֹדוּךָ עַמִּים | אֱלֹהִים יוֹדוּךָ עַמִּים כֻּלָּם:
יִשְׂמְחוּ וִירַנְּנוּ לְאֻמִּים כִּי־תִשְׁפֹּט עַמִּים מִישֹׁר וּלְאֻמִּים
| בָּאָרֶץ תַּנְחֵם סֶלָה: יוֹדוּךָ עַמִּים | אֱלֹהִים יוֹדוּךָ עַמִּים
כֻּלָּם: אֶרֶץ נָתְנָה יְבוּלָהּ יְבָרְכֵנוּ אֱלֹהִים אֱלֹהֵינוּ:
יְבָרְכֵנוּ אֱלֹהִים וְיִירְאוּ אוֹתוֹ כָּל־אַפְסֵי־אָרֶץ:

Fine

voice of the petitioner becomes plural.
She no longer asks for herself alone, but
for herself and her husband ("be gracious
to us and bless us"). This personal favor,
the gift of a child, for which they ask, is
not a gift for them alone. The birth of a
child is cause for global rejoicing, global
exultation. All people would then praise
God. The gift of a child enriches the
couple, God, and the world.

"May the earth yield its produce." In
this context "the earth" can refer to the
woman, and "its produce," to her child.

This prayer is to be said by a married woman after the Silent Prayer and before the final meditation, "May The One Who Makes Peace," on days when Tahanun is said.

MAY IT BE Your will, Lord my God and God of my forebears, to grant me today a day of wonder and livelihood. Remember me for good and think of me with compassion and protection, as is Your wont. Grant me a son: proper, righteous, diligent, fearing the Lord. Grant me a decent lot, a fair reward, and the good fortune to merit the world to come. May I be so blessed to hear only of life's goodness and sweetness. Give me fullness of days, and a long life with blessings of peace, contentment, and security; wisdom, knowledge, and understanding; pleasure, graciousness, and mercy—both with You in all Your majesty and with everyone whom I chance to meet. Direct my heart so that I might love You and fear You. Turn my heart so that I will do Your bidding wholeheartedly. May my portion be with the righteous. May I be sated with Your goodness. Deal kindly with me and mercifully, as becomes You.

Blessed are You who hears our prayers.

Once again the instructions for the petitioner are also instructive for us. We see here the assumption that women prayed every day, using a liturgy that incorporated the standard daily *Amidah*. But even more, women were expected to know the intricate rules of when a special supplemental, supplicatory prayer (*Tahanun*) is recited. Clearly, this prayer book

and the focused sentiments it reflects represent only one segment of an Italian Jewish woman's spiritual life. Indeed, prayer books of the daily liturgy from the sixteenth century written in Hebrew letters but translated into Italian for use by women have been preserved. By the eighteenth century, Jewish women could be expected to read the Latin alphabet (hence

תפלה che si dee dire da ogni Donna Maritata in que'
giorni ne' quali vi sia תחנה , e dee dirsi dopo il שמנה עשרה
prima di fare עשה שלום .

יְהִי רָצוֹן מִלְפָנֶיךָ יְיָ אֱלֹקַי וֵאלֹקֵי אֲבוֹתַי שֶׁתִּתֶּן־לִי
הַיּוֹם הַזֶּה מַתָּנָה טוֹבָה וּפַרְנָסָה טוֹבָה, וְזָכְרֵנִי בְּזִכָּרוֹן
טוֹב לְפָנֶיךָ וּפָקְדֵנִי בִּפְקֻדַּת יְשׁוּעָה וְרַחֲמִים לְמַעַן
שִׁמְךָ הַגָּדוֹל, וְתִתֶּן־לִי בֵּן הָגוּן זָכָר יָשָׁר צַדִּיק וִירֵא
שָׁמַיִם בַּסֵּתֶר וּבַגָּלוּי, וְתִתֶּן־לִי חֵלֶק טוֹב וְשָׂכָר טוֹב
וּמַזָּל טוֹב כְּדֵי שֶׁאֶזְכֶּה לְחַיֵּי הָעוֹלָם הַבָּא, וְתַשְׁמִיעֵנִי
שָׁמַע טוֹב וּתְבַשְּׂרֵנִי בְּשׂוֹרוֹת טוֹבוֹת, וְתִתֶּן־לִי אֹרֶךְ
יָמִים וּשְׁנוֹת חַיִּים וְשַׁלְוָה וְהַשְׁקֵט נָבְטַח וְחָכְמָה וְדַעַת
וּבִינָה וְחֵן וְחֶסֶד וְרַחֲמִים לְפָנֶיךָ וְלִפְנֵי כִסֵּא כְבוֹדֶךָ
וְלִפְנֵי כָל־הַבְּרִיּוֹת שֶׁרוֹאִין אֶת־פָנַי, וְיַחֵד לְבָבִי
לְאַהֲבָה וּלְיִרְאָה אֶת־שְׁמֶךָ וְהַט לִבִּי לַעֲשׂוֹת רְצוֹנְךָ
בְּלֵבָב שָׁלֵם, וְתֵן חֶלְקִי עִם הַצַּדִּיקִים וְשַׂבְּעֵנִי מִטּוּבְךָ
וְרַחֵם עָלַי כִּישׁוּעָתֶךָ לְמַעַן שִׁמְךָ הַגָּדוֹל. בָּרוּךְ אַתָּה יְיָ
שׁוֹמֵעַ תְּפִלָּה:

obviating the need to write Italian in
Hebrew letters) and to be able to understand a modest amount of liturgical Hebrew (hence diluting the need to
translate). What is fascinating is the
expectation throughout the centuries that
Italian women should learn to read Hebrew and to *davven* regularly.

Amid the by-now anticipated litany of
requests for healthy children, a good life,
a peaceful, long, and comfortable life, the
petitioner inserts a novel dimension: a
request for wisdom, understanding, and
knowledge. Whereas earlier these at-
tributes were judged to be meritorious
and desirable for her *sons*, they are now
desired by her, as well.

RULER of the Universe, forgive all my sins, wipe away all my failings, remove all my transgressions. Heal me, God, and I will be healed, save me and I shall be saved, for You, God, are the source of my song. Open my eyes to Your commandments. Subdue all my enemies, all my opponents, all my pursuers so that they may not rise up again. Tread upon their cherished places. Sustain me, for You shall be victorious over all of them. Destroy, disrupt, and disperse all those who rise against me, all those who conspire and counsel against me. Silence those who would speak ill of me. Save me from harsh judgment and from a vengeful adversary, whether he be Jew or non-Jew. Save me from captivity, from the sword, from exile, from horrible disease, and the sufferings of the grave; from bad advice, and from those who are insolent, from vicious people and corrupt companions; from destructive forces, from misfortune, from evil times that continually threaten to burst upon us, and from evil machinations.

Deal kindly and graciously with me and I will bless Your name forever; I will thank You all the days of my life. Fill my hours with peace and prosperity and honorable reputation. Grant me a peaceful death. Let it serve as atonement for all my sins and let my soul rest in the bond of life. Cleanse me on the day of judgment; be gracious to me on the day of reckoning. Dismiss any evil counsel, set in my heart only wise advice. Let all the visions and dreams that I dreamt and that others dreamt about me be turned to good. May the priestly blessing come true for me. Help me to succeed in my efforts and my dreams. For You hear every prayer. Blessed be the One who hears prayer.

This prayer focuses exclusively on the petitioner herself, not as bride, wife, or mother, but as a creature of God, alone in the world, struggling against sin and fear, beseeching God to protect her and grant her peace both in life and death. Some of this petition is taken from the daily morning prayers.

רִבּוֹן כָּל־הָעוֹלָמִים סְלַח לְכָל־חַטֹּאתַי וּמְחַל־לִי
עַל־כָּל־פְּשָׁעַי וְכַפֶּר־לִי עַל־כָּל־עֲוֹנוֹתַי, רְפָאֵנִי יְיָ
וְאֵרָפֵא הוֹשִׁיעֵנִי וְאִוָּשֵׁעָה כִּי תְהִלָּתִי אַתָּה, וְהָאֵר עֵינַי
בְּמִצְוֹתֶיךָ וְתַכְנִיעַ אֶת־כָּל־אֹיְבַי וְשׂטְנַי וְרֹדְפַי וְעוֹיְנַי
תַּחַת כַּפּוֹת רַגְלַי וְקַיֵּם־בִּי וְאַתָּה עַל בָּמוֹתֵימוֹ תִדְרֹךְ.
וּשְׁבוֹר וּגְעוֹר וּמְגוֹר אֶת־כָּל־הַקָּמִים עָלַי וְהַחוֹשְׁבִים
וְהַיּוֹעֲצִים עָלַי רָעָה וּסְתוֹם פִּי־דוֹבְרֵי רָעָתִי הַצִּילֵנִי
מִדִּין קָשֶׁה וּמִבַּעַל דִּין קָשֶׁה בֵּין שֶׁהוּא בֶּן־בְּרִית וּבֵין
שֶׁאֵינוֹ בֶּן־בְּרִית וְהַצִּילֵנִי מִשֶּׁבִי וּמֵחֶרֶב וּמִגָּלוּת
וּמֵחָלָאִים רָעִים וּמֵחִבּוּט הַקֶּבֶר וּמֵעֲצוֹת רָעוֹת וּמֵעַזֵּי
פָנִים וּמֵאָדָם רָע וּמֵחָבֵר רָע וּמִשָּׂטָן הַמַּשְׁחִית וּמִפֶּגַע
רָע וּמִשָּׁעוֹת רָעוֹת הַמִּתְרַגְּשׁוֹת וּבָאוֹת לָעוֹלָם,
וּמֵהִרְהוּרִים רָעִים עֲשֵׂה עִמִּי חֵן וָחֶסֶד וַאֲבָרְכָה שִׁמְךָ
לְעוֹלָם וָעֶד, וְאוֹדְךָ כָּל־יְמֵי חַיַּי וּבְשָׁלוֹם תְּמַלֵּא מִסְפַּר
יָמַי וּבְחַיִּים טוֹבִים וּבְשֵׁם טוֹב וּבְמִיתָה טוֹבָה וּתְהֵא
מִיתָתִי כַּפָּרָה עַל־כָּל־עֲוֹנוֹתַי וְתָנוּחַ נַפְשִׁי בִּצְרוֹר
הַחַיִּים וְנַקֵּנִי בְּיוֹם הַדִּין וְצַדְּקֵנִי בְּיוֹם הַמִּשְׁפָּט וְהָפֵר
עֲצַת רָעִים וְתִטַּע בְּלִבִּי עֵצוֹת טוֹבוֹת וְתֵיטִיב לִי עַל־
כָּל־הַחֶזְיוֹנוֹת וְכָל־הַחֲלוֹמוֹת שֶׁחָלַמְתִּי אֲנִי לְעַצְמִי
וְשֶׁחָלְמוּ אֲחֵרִים עָלַי וְהָבֹא עָלַי בִּרְכוֹת כֹּהֲנִים וְהַצְלַח
דְּרָכַי וּמַחְשְׁבוֹתַי כִּי אַתָּה שׁוֹמֵעַ תְּפִלַּת כָּל־פֶּה בָּרוּךְ
שׁוֹמֵעַ תְּפִלָּה:

Prayers to Be Recited on Days *Tahanun* Is Said

MAY IT BE Your will, God of all the hosts, Who sits enthroned upon the cherubim, that You receive my prayers, warmly and willingly. Open for me the gates of heaven, the gates of repentance, the gates of paradise, the gates of righteousness, the gates of blessing, and the gates of prayer. Just as You heard the prayers of Abraham our father on Mount Moriah, and the prayer of Isaac his son when he was bound upon the altar; the prayer of Jacob at Beth El, and the prayer of our ancestors by the Red Sea; the prayer of Moses at Horeb, and the prayer of Aaron amidst his Temple service; the prayer of Pinhas as he rose to lead the people, the prayer of Joshua at Gilgal, and the prayer of Samuel at Mizpah; the prayer of David and Solomon his son in the holy city of Jerusalem, and the prayer of Elijah on Mount Carmel; the prayer of Elisha at Jericho, and the prayer of Jonah in the belly of the whale; the prayer of Hezekiah when he was sick, and the prayer of Hananiah, Mishael,

(continued)

Access to heaven, as you might imagine, is not random and whimsical, but orderly and directed. Prayers and souls ascend and, depending upon their nature, gain entry through appropriate gates and windows. Here the petitioner seeks a diver-

sity of avenues, hoping that at least one, and perhaps even all, will allow her petition through (based on *Berakhot* 32b).

By reciting a virtual catalog of successful prayer stories, piling precedent upon precedent, each more miraculous than the

יְהִי רָצוֹן מִלְפָנֶיךָ יְיָ אֱלֹהֵי הַצְּבָאוֹת יוֹשֵׁב הַכְּרוּבִים
שֶׁתְּקַבֵּל בְּרַחֲמִים וּבְרָצוֹן אֶת־תְּפִלָּתִי וְתִפְתַּח־לִי
שַׁעֲרֵי שָׁמַיִם וְשַׁעֲרֵי תְשׁוּבָה וְשַׁעֲרֵי גַן־עֵדֶן וְשַׁעֲרֵי
צְדָקָה וְשַׁעֲרֵי בְרָכָה וְשַׁעֲרֵי תְפִלָּה כְּמוֹ שֶׁשָּׁמַעְתָּ
תְּפִלַּת אַבְרָהָם אָבִינוּ בְּהַר הַמּוֹרִיָּה וּתְפִלַּת יִצְחָק בְּנוֹ
עַל גַּבֵּי הַמִּזְבֵּחַ וּתְפִלַּת יַעֲקֹב בְּבֵית־אֵל וּתְפִלַּת
אֲבוֹתֵינוּ עַל יָם־סוּף וּתְפִלַּת מֹשֶׁה בְּחוֹרֵב וּתְפִלַּת
אַהֲרֹן בַּמַּחְתָּה וּתְפִלַּת פִּינְחָס בְּקוּמוֹ מִתּוֹךְ הָעֵדָה
וּתְפִלַּת יְהוֹשֻׁעַ בַּגִּלְגָּל וּתְפִלַּת שְׁמוּאֵל בַּמִּצְפָּה וּתְפִלַּת
דָּוִד וּשְׁלֹמֹה בְנוֹ בִּירוּשָׁלַם וּתְפִלַּת אֵלִיָּהוּ בְּהַר
הַכַּרְמֶל וּתְפִלַּת אֱלִישָׁע בִּירִיחוֹ וּתְפִלַּת יוֹנָה בִּמְעֵי
הַדָּגָה וּתְפִלַּת חִזְקִיָּהוּ בְּחָלְיוֹ וּתְפִלַּת חֲנַנְיָה מִישָׁאֵל
וַעֲזַרְיָה בְּתוֹךְ כִּבְשַׁן הָאֵשׁ וּתְפִלַּת דָּנִיֵּאל בְּגוֹב אֲרָיוֹת
וּתְפִלַּת מָרְדְּכַי וְאֶסְתֵּר בְּשׁוּשַׁן הַבִּירָה וּתְפִלַּת עֶזְרָא

(continued)

current request, the petitioner shows how natural, how easy, how right it would be for God to grant her desire, a son.

According to some traditions, the idyllic world of the messianic age will be preceded by a wrenching upheaval of the natural and social order. This upheaval is called the birth pangs of the messiah. The desire to see the messianic age dawn is tempered by a desire not to be there when it happens. Such a sentiment is reflected in the last line of this prayer.

and Azariah from the fiery furnace; the prayer of Daniel in the lion's den, and the prayer of Mordecai and Esther in the capital city of Shushan; the prayer of Ezra in exile, and the prayer of all the righteous and the pure, so may You hear my voice, the pleas of Your maid servant {Baila Yudita, daughter of Rahel}. Give me a son who is strong and righteous and proper and good. Banish from me evil thoughts and evil inclinations. Place within me the fear of You. May I merit a life of Torah and good deeds. May I, today and always, be seen by You and all whom I encounter as one full of goodness and mercy and kindness. Spare me from evil judgment and the punishment of hell, from the sufferings beyond the grave, and from the birth pains of the Messiah. Deal kindly with me. Amen.

Conclusion of this prayer

בְּגוֹלָה וּתְפִלַּת כָּל־הַצַּדִּיקִים וְהַתְּמִימִים בֶּן תִּשְׁמַע

קוֹלִי מִמֶּנִּי אֲמָתֶךָ וְתִתֶּן־לִי בֵּן זָכָר יָשָׁר

חָסִיד הָגוּן וְצַדִּיק וְהָסֵר מִמֶּנִּי לֵב רָע וְיֵצֶר רָע וְתֵן

בְּלִבִּי יִרְאָתֶךָ וְתַזְכֵּנִי לְתוֹרָה וּלְמַעֲשִׂים טוֹבִים וּתְנֵנִי

הַיּוֹם וּבְכָל־יוֹם לְחֵן וּלְחֶסֶד וּלְרַחֲמִים בְּעֵינֶיךָ וּבְעֵינֵי

כָל־רוֹאַי וְתַצִּילֵנִי מִדִּין קָשֶׁה וּמְדִינָה שֶׁל גֵּהִינָם

וּמֵחִבּוּט הַקֶּבֶר וּמֵחֶבְלֵי מָשִׁיחַ וְתִגְמְלֵנִי חֲסָדִים טוֹבִים

אָמֵן:

Fine di questa Orazione

Prayers to Be Recited on Days *Tahanun* Is Not Said

A married woman says this on the days when Tahanun *is not said, inserting the following in the Silent Prayer before the final meditation, "May The One Who Makes Peace."*

MAY IT BE Your will, Lord my God and God of my forebears, that this moment, as I stand before You petitioning You on behalf of myself and all members of my household, be a time of acceptance, a time of attentiveness. I call to You and You answer me. I plead with You, and You respond, granting that one day I will bear a son who is good and righteous and proper, fearing heaven both in private and in public. Command Your angels, those assigned to the affairs of humankind, to be with me as helpers, guides, and protectors. Incline the hearts of all I engage to my will. Shape their desires to match my desires. Thwart the designs of my enemies and make all my requests be for

(continued)

Tahanun is a prayer of contrition, humility, and petition. On the days when it is not said, the additional personal prayer avoids these heavy sentiments.

After asking for a son, the petitioner invites God's company, God's guidance in all her endeavors, her thoughts, her deeds, and her progress. This prayer is

תפלה che dee dirsi dalla Donna maritata in que giorni ne'quali non si dice תחנה , e dee dirsi dopo שמנה עשרה prima di fare עשה שלום .

יְהִי רָצוֹן מִלְפָנֶיךָ יְיָ אֱלֹקַי וֵאלֹקֵי אֲבוֹתַי שֶׁתְּהֵא שָׁעָה זוֹ שֶׁאֲנִי עוֹמֶדֶת לְהִתְפַּלֵּל עַל נַפְשִׁי וְעַל נַפְשׁוֹת בֵּיתִי שָׁעַת רָצוֹן וְשָׁעַת הַאֲזָנָה אֶקְרָאֶךָ וְתַעֲנֵנִי אֶעְתַּר־לָךְ וְתֵעָתֶר־לִי לְזַכּוֹת אוֹתִי שֶׁאֵלֵד בֵּן זָכָר הָגוּן יָשָׁר וְצַדִּיק יְרֵא שָׁמַיִם בַּסֵתֶר וּבַגָּלוּי, וְצַוֵּה לְמַלְאָכֶיךָ הַמְמוּנִים עַל־עִנְיָנֵי בְּנֵי אָדָם שֶׁיִהְיוּ עִמִּי לַעֲזוֹר וּלְהוֹשִׁיעַ וּלְהַצִּיל וְהַטֵּה כָּל־לִבּוֹת בְּנֵי־אָדָם שֶׁיֵשׁ לִי עֵסֶק עִמָּהֶם לְכָל־אֲשֶׁר אֶחְפּוֹץ וְהָשֵׁב רְצוֹנָם לְכָל־ אֲשֶׁר אֶרְצֶה וּבַטֵּל מַחְשְׁבוֹת שׂוֹנְאַי וַהֲפוֹךְ כָּל־

(continued)

written in a most independent voice. There is no mention of her husband, no request to be supported by family. Indeed, she prays that *she* may be a source of blessing, that her judgment and her designs be wise and abiding. She turns only to God for guidance, hope, and strength.

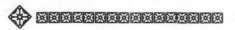

good, as it is written, "He will give you as your heart desires and all your counsel He·will fulfill" (Psalm 20:5). Be with me in my deliberations, and guide my hands as I work. Enlighten me; show me the way. May all that I do provide blessing. Keep me from turning in need to others. Let me rely only upon You and Your plentiful and bountiful hand. Lift me from the dust of my poverty. Raise me from the refuse of the lowest. Support me with Your strong right hand full of blessings and deal kindly with me. Blessed is the One who deals kindly with His people Israel. Amen.

Conclusion

מִשְׁאֲלוֹתַי לְטוֹבָה כַּכָּתוּב יִתֶּן־לְךָ כִלְבָבֶךָ וְכָל־עֲצָתְךָ
יְמַלֵּא וְתִהְיֶה עִם לְבָבִי בְּעֵת מַחְשְׁבוֹתַי וְעִם יָדַי בְּעֵת
מַעֲבָדַי וְתַשְׂכִּילֵנִי וְתוֹרֵנִי בְּכָל־מַהֲלָכִי וְתִשְׁלַח בְּרָכָה
בְּכָל־מַעֲשֵׂי יָדַי וְאַל תַּצְרִיכֵנִי לִידֵי מַתְּנַת בָּשָׂר וָדָם
אֶלָּא לְיָדְךָ הַמְּלֵאָה וְהָרְחָבָה וּמֵעָפָר עָנְיִי תְּקִימֵנִי
וּמֵאַשְׁפוֹת דַּלּוּתִי תְּרִימֵנִי וְתִסְעָדֵנִי בִּימִין בִּרְכוֹתֶיךָ
וְתִגְמְלֵנִי חֲסָדִים טוֹבִים בָּרוּךְ הַגּוֹמֵל חֲסָדִים טוֹבִים
לְעַמּוֹ יִשְׂרָאֵל, אָמֵן:

Fine

Prayers to Be Said during the First Forty Days of Pregnancy

A prayer to be recited by a married woman during the first forty days of her pregnancy. It is to be added after the Sh'moneh Esrai *and before the concluding meditation, "May The One Who Makes Peace."*

LORD my God and God of my forebears, bestow upon me Your greatest mercies, so that the child that I carry within me may be a pure, innocent son. May he be good and kind and sacred, to serve as a blessing. Let him be a shining light to all Israel, illuminating Your Torah. Amen. So may it be Your will.

Conclusion of the prayer

According to tradition, the gender of a child *in utero* is not determined until the forty-first day of pregnancy. Throughout the first forty days, the petitioner can still hope to affect the sex of the child. After the fortieth day, the gender is immutably

תפלה che dee dirsi dalla donna maritata nelli primi quaranta giorni della sua Gravidanza dopo שמנה עשרה prima di fare עשה שלום .

יְהִי רָצוֹן מִלְּפָנֶיךָ יְיָ אֱלֹקַי וֵאלֹקֵי אֲבוֹתַי שֶׁתְּזַכֵּנִי בְּרַחֲמֶיךָ הָרַבִּים שֶׁהַוְּלָד שֶׁבְּמֵעַי יִהְיֶה בֶּן זָכָר תָּמִים וְשֶׁיִּהְיֶה צַדִּיק חָסִיד וְקָדוֹשׁ לִבְרָכָה, וְיִהְיֶה מֵאִיר עֵינֵי יִשְׂרָאֵל בְּתוֹרָתֶךָ: אָמֵן כֵּן יְהִי רָצוֹן:

Fine dell' Orazione

determined. To request a son after the fortieth day is prohibited, for to do so would be to recite a *tefillat shav,* a prayer uttered in vain.

But to request a son within the formative period is fair play.

Prayers to Be Said during the Entire Pregnancy

A prayer to be recited by every woman every day of her pregnancy. It is to be added after the Sh'moneh Esrai *and before the final meditation, "May The One Who Makes Peace."*

LORD of the Universe, Ruler of the Hosts, all creatures look hopefully to You. In their time of trouble they look to You for salvation. And even though I am not worthy to come before You with my prayer, I harden my resolve and approach to humbly place my request before You. Just as You remembered Sarah, heeded Rebecca, saw Leah's sorrow, and did not forget Rachel, just as You listened to the voice of all the righteous women when they turned to You, so may You hear the sound of my plea and send the redeeming angel to protect me and to help me throughout my pregnancy.

(continued)

Once again the petitioner places before God a brief record of divine mercy and responsiveness, as if to say: If it was done once, twice, four times before, surely it can be done again for me. And in this case there is an immediate, specific identity between the models from the past, our matriachs and their prayers, and the petitioner and her prayer.

Conception is only a beginning. The path to a successful delivery is fraught with dangers for both mother and child. In this prayer, one of the longest in the book, the petitioner asks for physical and spiritual well-being, both for herself and throughout her child's life.

Deliver, in Hebrew (פלט), as in English, means both to rescue and to give

תפלה che dirsi debbe dalla Donna in tutti i giorni
della sua Gravidanza dopo il שמנה עשרה prima di
fare עשה שלום .

רִבּוֹן הָעוֹלָמִים אֲדוֹן הַצְּבָאוֹת עֵינֵי כֹל אֵלֶיךָ יְשַׂבֵּרוּ
וּבְעֵת צָרָה לְךָ יְשַׁוֵּעוּ, וְעִם כִּי אֵינִי כְּדַאִית לָבוֹא
לְפָנֶיךָ בִּתְפִלָּתִי שַׂמְתִּי פָנַי כַּחַלָּמִישׁ וּבָאתִי לְהַפִּיל
תְּחִנָּתִי לְפָנֶיךָ שֶׁכְּשֵׁם שֶׁפָּקַדְתָּ אֶת־שָׂרָה וְנֶעְתַּרְתָּ
לְרִבְקָה וְרָאִיתָ בָּעֳנִי לֵאָה וְזָכַרְתָּ אֶת רָחֵל וְשָׁמַעְתָּ
לְקוֹל הַצִּדְקָנִיּוֹת בְּשַׁוְעָם אֵלֶיךָ כֵּן תִּשְׁמַע לְקוֹל שַׁוְעִי
וְתִשְׁלַח מַלְאַךְ הַגּוֹאֵל לְסָמְכֵנִי וּלְעָזְרֵנִי בְּעֵת הֵרָיוֹנִי
זֶה.

(continued)

birth. Given the number of Hebrew words for *salvation*, it is noteworthy that *deliver* is the one chosen for this context. Interestingly, the word also appears in Psalm 71 in a verse quoted on page 55. But in the quotation *deliver* was changed to *save*. Why did the one who crafted these prayers alter the biblical text? Perhaps because earlier the petitioner was not yet pregnant. To use *deliver* in a petition to become pregnant might, at best, be seen as premature and, at worst, as mocking.

The use of the word *hour* reveals a subtle belief in the power of the stars. The time of one's birth, it was believed, largely determined the quality of one's life.

In accordance with Your graciousness, save me from all harm, sickness, hurt, disability, and pain. Be gracious to me so that the child I carry not be malformed, and grant me an unconditional gift from Your finest treasure trove. Listen to the prayer that springs from the deepest recesses of my heart, and let the child I bear within me be righteous and good and proper. May he stand before You with his wisdom, his knowledge of Torah, and the legacy of his kindness. May he forever be prepared to do Your work and to fear You. May he be loved and cherished by all in the world above and in this world below. Strengthen me and gird me so I shall not miscarry. Make the time of this birth be propitious so that I shall bring forth into the light of the world a child of perfect body and limb.

Send me Your help from the holy place so that I may be protected by Your abundant mercy, in accordance with Your nature. Save me, deliver me, let me share the fate of righteous women who did not suffer the punishment of Eve. But if I do not merit this goodness, please do this for Your own sake. May the child that I bear be dedicated to Your work and to fearing Your great name. Make his entire being flow with Torah, as You did with Abraham, Your

(continued)

וּלְמַעַן חַסְדְּךָ תּוֹשִׁיעֵנִי וְתַצִּילֵנִי מִכָּל־פֶּגַע רָע
וּמַחֲלָה וּמִכְאוֹב וּמַדְוֶה וָעֶצֶב. וְחָנֵּנִי שֶׁלֹּא יִהְיֶה הַוָּלָד
שֶׁבְּמֵעַי סַנְדָּל וְחָנֵּנִי מֵאוֹצַר הַטּוֹב שֶׁל מַתְּנַת חִנָּם
וּשְׁמַע תְּפִלָּתִי זֹאת הַבָּאָה מִקִּירוֹת לִבִּי לְהִתְחַנֵּן
לְפָנֶיךָ שֶׁיִּהְיֶה הַוָּלָד שֶׁבְּמֵעַי צַדִּיק יָשָׁר הָגוּן לַעֲמוֹד
לְפָנֶיךָ בְּחָכְמָתוֹ וּבְתוֹרָתוֹ וּבְמַעֲשָׂיו הַטּוֹבִים וְיִהְיֶה
מוּכָן כָּל־יָמָיו לַעֲבוֹדָתְךָ וּלְיִרְאָתֶךָ, וְיִהְיֶה אָהוּב
וְנֶחְמָד בְּעֵינֵי הַכֹּל בֵּין לְמַעְלָה בֵּין לְמַטָּה וּתְחַזְּקֵנִי
וּתְאַמְּצֵנִי לְבַל אַפִּילֵנוּ מִמֵּעַי, וּבְעֵת לִדְתִּי הַזְמֵן־לִי
שָׁעָה טוֹבָה שֶׁאוֹצִיאֵנוּ לְאוֹר הָעוֹלָם וְשֶׁיִּהְיֶה שָׁלֵם
בְּגוּפוֹ וְאֵבָרָיו.

וּשְׁלַח עֶזְרְךָ מִקֹּדֶשׁ לְהַשְׁגִּיחַ עָלַי בְּרֹב חֲסָדֶיךָ
לְמַעַן שִׁמְךָ הַגָּדוֹל וּתְחַלְּצֵנִי וּתְפַלְּטֵנִי כְּמִשְׁפַּט כָּל־
הַצַּדְקָנִיּוֹת אֲשֶׁר לֹא הָיוּ בְּפִתְקָה שֶׁל חַנָּה, וְאִם אֵין
בִּי זְכוּת עֲשֵׂה לְמַעַן שִׁמְךָ הַגָּדוֹל הַגִּבּוֹר וְהַנּוֹרָא,
וְהַוָּלָד שֶׁאֵלֵד הָכִינֵהוּ לַעֲבוֹד אוֹתְךָ וּלְיִרְאָה אֶת־
שְׁמֶךָ וַעֲשֵׂה לוֹ שְׁתֵּי כְּלָיוֹתָיו נוֹבְעוֹת תּוֹרָה כְּמוֹ
שֶׁעָשִׂיתָ לְאַבְרָהָם יְחִידְךָ, וְהַזְמֵן־לוֹ־שָׁעָה רְאוּיָה

(continued)

cherished one. May the hour of his birth be one which endows propriety, strength, and dignity so that he may serve You well. May the hour of his birth assure him prosperity so that he shall not be in need of any other living creature, not of their gifts and not of their loans. As for me, Your maidservant, prepare my breasts full of milk so that I may nurse the child as much as he needs, so that he may not suffer hunger. Be gracious to me so that I will be able to raise my child with love for You and with dedication to Your holy work. Give my husband a good life, and a long life, a life of peace, a life of wealth and honor, a life of decency, a life free of disgrace and indignity, a life in which You have fulfilled all our noble requests. Let us gain our livelihood directly from Your expansive, generous hand, without travail or undue exertion, with honor and without shame, with inner peace spared of trouble, with abundance and achievement, safe from poverty and loss. May all our efforts succeed. Be gracious unto me and listen to my prayer, for You listen to the prayer of all who call upon You. Blessed be the One who listens to prayer.

Conclusion of this prayer

וּנְכוֹנָה וְכֹחַ וְחַיִל לַעֲבוֹד אוֹתָךְ, שְׁעַת פַּרְנָסָה שֶׁלֹּא
יִצְטָרֵךְ לַבְּרִיּוֹת מִשׁוּם דָּבָר לֹא מִמַּתְּנָתָם וְלֹא
מֵהַלְוָאָתָם, וְלִי אֲנִי אֲמָתְךָ הַזְּמֵן בְּשָׁדֵי חָלָב מַסְפִּיק
לְהָנִיק אֶת כָּל־צָרְכּוֹ וְלֹא יֶחְסַר מַאֲכָלוֹ, וְחָנֵּנִי
שֶׁאוּכַל לְגַדֵּל אֶת אוֹתוֹ לְאַהֲבָתָךְ וּלְיִרְאָתָךְ וּלְתַלְמוּד
תוֹרָתָךְ וּלְקִיּוּם מִצְוֹתֶיךָ וַעֲבוֹדָתֶךָ, וּלְבַעֲלִי תֵּן חַיִּים
טוֹבִים וַאֲרֻכִּים, חַיִּים שֶׁל שַׁלְוָה, חַיִּים שֶׁל עֹשֶׁר
וְכָבוֹד, חַיִּים שֶׁל יִרְאַת חֵטְא, חַיִּים שֶׁלֹּא יִהְיֶה בָּהֶם
בּוּשָׁה וּכְלִימָה, חַיִּים שֶׁתְּמַלֵּא כָּל־מִשְׁאֲלוֹת לִבֵּנוּ
לְטוֹבָה, וְתַזְמִין לָנוּ כָּל־פַּרְנָסָתֵנוּ מִיָּדְךָ הָרְחָבָה
וְהַמְּלֵאָה בְּלִי ·טֹרַח וְעָמָל בְּכָבוֹד וְלֹא בְּבִזּוּי, בְּנַחַת
וְלֹא בְּצַעַר, בְּרֶוַח וְהַצְלָחָה וְלֹא כְּהֶפְסֵד וְתַצְלִיחֵנוּ
בְּכָל־מַעֲשֵׂה יָדֵינוּ וְחָנֵּנִי וּשְׁמַע תְּפִלָּתִי כִּי אַתָּה שֹׁמֵעַ
תְּפִלַּת כָּל־פֶּה. בָּרוּךְ שֹׁמֵעַ תְּפִלָּה:

Fine di questa Orazione

Prayers to Be Said during the Seventh Month of Pregnancy

When a woman enters the seventh month of her pregnancy, she must fast and give charity to the poor according to her means. And every day until she gives birth, she must recite this prayer after the Sh'moneh Esrai *and before "May The One Who Makes Peace."*

LORD our God and God of our forebears, may it be Your will that I [Baila Yudita, daughter of Rahel] easily suffer the strains of my pregnancy. Continually grant me stamina throughout the pregnancy so that the baby's strength may not fail, nor mine, in any way. Save me from the judgment visited upon Eve, and at the time of birth when the days of my pregnancy are complete, let me not be wracked by the pains of labor. Let the child be born speedily, and may I give birth easily, as naturally as a chicken and quickly, without any harm either to me or to the child. Let the child be born when the time is right, at a propitious moment, so he may enjoy a full life of peace, health, and pleasantness, of goodness, prosperity, and honor. May I not give

(continued)

Pain in childbirth is, according to Torah, a punishment visited upon Eve for transgressing God's decree concerning the Tree of Knowledge. The concept of פתקה, the judgment—or more precisely the writ of punishment—comes from the talmudic tractate of *Sotah 12a*. We are not told, however, the precise act that defined Eve's

Quando la Donna entra nel Settimo Mese della
sua gravidanza dee disporsi a fare un Digiuno,
e dee far charità a Poveri secondo la sua possibilità,
ed ogni giorno Sino il giorno del Parto dee dire dire dopo
il שמנה עשרה prima di fare עשה שלום questa תפילה .

יְהִי רָצוֹן מִלְפָנֶיךָ יְיָ אֱלֹקֵינוּ וֵאלֹקֵי אֲבוֹתֵינוּ שֶׁתִּסְתַּכֵּל
מֵעָלַי בִּילָה יוּדִיטָא בַּת רָחֵל אֶת־צַעַר עֻבּוּרִי וְתוֹסִיף לִי כֹּחַ
כָּל־יְמֵי עֻבּוּרִי שֶׁלֹא יוּתַשׁ כֹּחַ הָעֻבָּר וְלֹא כֹחִי בְּשׁוּם
דָּבָר שֶׁבָּעוֹלָם. וְתַצִּיל אוֹתִי מִפֶּתְקָה שֶׁל חַוָּה. וּבְעֵת
לֵדְתִּי כִּי יִמְלְאוּ יָמַי לָלֶדֶת לֹא יֵהָפְכוּ עָלַי צִירֵי
הַלֵּידָה וְיֵצֵא הַוָּלָד לַאֲוֵיר הָעוֹלָם בְּרֶגַע קָטָן וְאֵלֵד
בְּנָקֵל כְּתַרְנְגוֹלֶת בְּקַלּוּת בְּלִי שׁוּם הֶזֵק לֹא לִי וְלֹא
לַוָּלָד. וְיִהְיֶה נוֹלָד בְּשָׁעָה טוֹבָה וּמַזָּל טוֹב לְחַיִּים
וּלְשָׁלוֹם וְלִבְרִיאוּת לְחֵן וּלְחֶסֶד לְעֹשֶׁר וְלִכָבוֹד.

(continued)

---

transgression. Was it because she gave the forbidden fruit to Adam and made him eat? (So thought Adam and the whole of western tradition—Genesis 3:12). Was it because she ate? (So thought Eve—Genesis 3:12) Why does it matter? Revealed in these two views are the differing values, the different import, assigned to

birth on Shabbat, causing others to transgress the laws of Shabbat for my sake. Fulfill all my requests graciously, generously, and mercifully, along with the requests of all Israel who bid Your mercy. Do not send me away from You empty. Amen. Selah.

In Your hand, Lord our God, is the key to life and to birth. This key is not given over into the hands of any angel. Therefore, remember Your graciousness and Your goodness, and remember me for life. Deal graciously and kindly with me, that I may give birth easily to a thriving child selected from the holy source, just as David sang in his psalms: "In distress I called on the Lord. The Lord answered me by setting me free. The Lord is with me, I have no fear. What can anyone do to me?" (Psalm 118:5–6). May the One who heard David's prayer at the time of his troubles, listen also to my prayer. Just as He answered our holy mothers Sarah, Rebecca, Rachel, Leah, Hannah, and all the righteous and pious women of Israel, so may He answer me. Amen. May the words of my mouth and the meditations of my heart be acceptable to You, Lord, my Rock and my Redeemer.

women's independent actions. One cannot easily find in tradition a recognition of the significance of woman's action, whether one woman alone, or in the company of women. Women's acts become meaningful in the eyes of tradition only when they involve men.

The curse of pain in childbirth was not directed at Eve alone, but at all her daughters throughout time. Yet, tradition tells us that one generation of women was spared: the generation of the righteous women of the Exodus. The petitioner therefore requests that she, too, regardless of merit, be granted such exclusion.

In the worldview reflected in this prayer book, God is assisted in the running of the world's affairs by a host of angels. Yet, three of life's secrets are

וְשֶׁלֹּא אֵלֵד בְּשַׁבָּת וְיִצְטָרְכוּ לְחַלֵּל שַׁבָּת בִּשְׁבִילִי.
וּתְמַלֵּא כָּל־מִשְׁאֲלוֹתַי בְּמִדָּה טוֹבָה יְשׁוּעָה וְרַחֲמִים
בְּקֶרֶב כָּל־יִשְׂרָאֵל הַצְּרִיכִים רַחֲמִים וְאַל תְּשִׁיבֵנִי
רֵיקָם מִלְּפָנֶיךָ אָמֵן סֶלָה וָעֶד. וּבְיָדְךָ יְיָ אֱלֹקֵינוּ
הַמַּפְתֵּחַ שֶׁל חַיָּה וְהַלֵּידָה שֶׁלֹּא נִמְסָרָה לְשׁוּם מַלְאָךְ
לָכֵן זְכוֹר בְּרַחֲמֶיךָ יְיָ בַחֲסָדֶיךָ וְזָכְרֵנִי לְחַיִּים וּפָקְדֵנִי
בִּישׁוּעָה וְרַחֲמִים וְאֵלֵד בְּרֶוַח זֶרַע שֶׁל קַיָּמָא מִסִּטְרָא
דִּקְדֻשָּׁא כְּמוֹ שֶׁזִּמֵּר דָּוִד בַּתְּהִלִּים מִן הַמֵּצַר קָרָאתִי
יָּהּ עָנָנִי בַמֶּרְחַב יָהּ: יְיָ לִי לֹא אִירָא מַה יַּעֲשֶׂה לִי
אָדָם: מִי שֶׁשָּׁמַע תְּפִלַּת דָּוִד בְּעֵת צָרוֹתָיו הוּא
יִשְׁמַע אֶת־תְּפִלָּתִי זֹאת וּכְמוֹ שֶׁעָנָה לְאִמּוֹתֵינוּ
הַקְּדוֹשׁוֹת שָׂרָה רִבְקָה רָחֵל וְלֵאָה וְחַנָּה וּלְכָל־
הַצַּדִּיקוֹת וְהַחֲסִידוֹת וְהַהֲגוּנוֹת הוּא יַעֲנֵנִי. אָמֵן: יִהְיוּ
לְרָצוֹן אִמְרֵי־פִי וְהֶגְיוֹן לִבִּי לְפָנֶיךָ יְיָ צוּרִי וְגוֹאֲלִי:

beyond the jurisdiction of angelic agency. One is the secret, or key, to the gift of life itself. For this, the petitioner requests God's unmediated, divine intervention.

The language quoted from Psalm 118:5 is more than a reference to God's beneficent answer in a time of need. In the Hebrew, distress (*meitzar,* מיצר), conjures up images of narrowness, tightness, confinement, the very conditions that must be overcome for a successful birth. Free (*merkhav,* מרחב) in Hebrew connotes vastness, spaciousness, roominess, the conditions necessary for a healthy birth. Far from being generic, this verse, placed here, reminds God of the specific task that lies ahead.

A PSALM of David. May the LORD answer you in time of trouble, may the God of Jacob be your strength.
May He send you help from His sanctuary,
sustaining you from Zion.
May He remember all your offerings and accept your sacrifices,
granting your heart's desires, fulfilling all your hopes.

We shall sing of Your victory,
we shall acclaim the glory of our God.
May the LORD fulfill all that you ask.
Now I know that the LORD delivers His anointed.
He will answer from His heavenly abode,
bringing victory with mighty deeds.
Some trust in chariots, others in horses,
but we honor the name of the LORD our God.
They stumble and fall, but we rise and stand firm.
O LORD, deliver us!
Answer us, O King, when we call.

Psalm 20

And then three times she says the following:

TO HEAR the groans of the prisoner, to release those condemned to death. To death those condemned to release, of the prisoner the groans to hear (Psalm 102:21).

לַמְנַצֵּחַ מִזְמוֹר לְדָוִד: יַעַנְךָ יְיָ בְּיוֹם צָרָה יְשַׂגֶּבְךָ שֵׁם | אֱלֹהֵי
יַעֲקֹב: יִשְׁלַח־עֶזְרְךָ מִקֹּדֶשׁ וּמִצִּיּוֹן יִסְעָדֶךָּ: יִזְכֹּר כָּל־מִנְחֹתֶיךָ
וְעוֹלָתְךָ יְדַשְּׁנֶה סֶלָה: יִתֶּן־לְךָ כִלְבָבֶךָ וְכָל־עֲצָתְךָ יְמַלֵּא: נְרַנְּנָה |
בִּישׁוּעָתֶךָ וּבְשֵׁם־אֱלֹהֵינוּ נִדְגֹּל יְמַלֵּא יְיָ כָּל־מִשְׁאֲלוֹתֶיךָ: עַתָּה
יָדַעְתִּי כִּי הוֹשִׁיעַ | יְיָ מְשִׁיחוֹ יַעֲנֵהוּ מִשְּׁמֵי קָדְשׁוֹ בִּגְבוּרוֹת יֵשַׁע
יְמִינוֹ: אֵלֶּה בָרֶכֶב וְאֵלֶּה בַסּוּסִים וַאֲנַחְנוּ בְּשֵׁם־יְיָ אֱלֹהֵינוּ נַזְכִּיר:
הֵמָּה כָּרְעוּ וְנָפָלוּ וַאֲנַחְנוּ קַּמְנוּ וַנִּתְעוֹדָד: יְיָ הוֹשִׁיעָה הַמֶּלֶךְ יַעֲנֵנוּ
בְיוֹם־קָרְאֵנוּ:

e poi dirà tre volte il seguente

לִשְׁמֹעַ אֶנְקַת אָסִיר לְפַתֵּחַ בְּנֵי תְמוּתָה: תְמוּתָה
בְּנֵי לְפַתֵּחַ אָסִיר אֶנְקַת לִשְׁמֹעַ:

Then say the following verses three times:

THEN ALL these courtiers of yours shall come down to me and bow low to me, saying, "Depart, you and all the people who follow you! And after that I will depart," and he left (Exodus 11:8).

And he left. I will depart and after that who follow you, people all the and you depart saying to me low bow and down to me come shall these courtiers of yours, then all.

Conclusion

The third trimester has begun. Thoughts focus, with increasing eagerness and anxiety, on the moment of childbirth itself. Superstitions and incantations are employed to ease and make safe the act of birth. Truly, women in labor are prisoners of their pain, groaning for release from the burden they carry. In an age without caesarean sections or curative antibiotics, birth all too often brought death. It was hoped that by reciting the verses, forward and backward, three times, the moment of birth would be quick, easy, and safe.

The verse from Exodus, which is recited three times, forward and backward, contains within it the word *depart* three times. Eighteen times the woman says *depart, leave, get out*. Eighteen times she

E poi dirà tre volte quello che segue

וְיֵרְדוּ כָל־עֲבָדֶיךָ אֵלֶּה אֵלַי וְהִשְׁתַּחֲווּ לִי לֵאמֹר צֵא
אַתָּה וְכָל־הָעָם אֲשֶׁר בְּרַגְלֶיךָ וְאַחֲרֵי־כֵן אֵצֵא וַיֵּצֵא:
וַיֵּצֵא אֵצֵא כֵן וְאַחֲרֵי בְּרַגְלֶיךָ אֲשֶׁר הָעָם וְכָל־אַתָּה
צֵא לֵאמֹר לִי וְהִשְׁתַּחֲווּ אֵלַי אֵלֶּה עֲבָדֶיךָ כָל־יֵרְדוּ:

Fine

calls upon the child to leave her womb when the time is right. Even as God guided the delivery of the children of Israel from slavery in *Mitzrayim* (Hebrew for Egypt), whose very name connotes confinement and narrowness, so the woman prays for God's guiding hand in the delivery of her child from the narrow place within her.

And, in an extension of the metaphor created by this prayer, we can see in the birth of a single child, a moment as monumental, as rich in potential, as consequential, as the birth of a chosen nation.

Prayers to Be Said during the Ninth Month of Pregnancy

A prayer to be said by a woman when she enters the ninth month of her pregnancy. It is to be inserted after the Sh'moneh Esrai *and before "May The One Who Makes Peace."*

I THANK the Lord with all my heart that I have carried the full nine months and that up to now He has spared me from all afflictions that could harm a pregnant woman and her child. Surely God's tenderness is unending. Again, I seek His kindness so He will be with me and support me when my child is pressing to be born, and so that He will give me strength to bring forth my child. Please, God, sustain me and I will be saved. Keep me from distress, allowing my child to emerge from me full of life and vigor. May neither he nor any part of his body suffer harm or disfigurement or loss or accident or pain or harm, disease or illness. Fill my breasts with milk enough to nurse him, and be gracious unto me so that I may be able to raise him to fear You and to do Your holy work. Send with him blessings, abundance, and success so that he may grow to be a prosperous man. For him, may my

(continued)

The journey is almost over. The woman thanks God for bringing her in health to this moment. But neither she, nor God, can rest yet. So despite her gratitude, the petitioner returns to her supplication.

And as before, she reminds God that the birth of a healthy child is as much a boon for God as for herself.

"Send with him. . . ." Every child is both a gift and a messenger from God. As

תפלה Che dee dirsi dalla Donna quando entra nel Nono
mese della sua Gravidanza dopo il שמנה עשרה prima
di fare עושה שלום .

אוֹדֶה יְיָ בְּכָל־לֵבָב כִּי בָאתִי בִּכְלָל תִּשְׁעָה יְרָחִים
וְעַד כֹּה הִצִּילַנִי מִפְּגָעִים רָעִים שֶׁיְּכוֹלִים לִפְגַּע
בְּאִשָּׁה הָרָה וּבְוַלְדָהּ. הַטּוֹב כִּי לֹא כָלוּ רַחֲמָיו אֲשֶׁר
עַל כֵּן אֲבַקֵּשׁ רַחֲמִים מִמֶּנּוּ שֶׁיִּסְעָדֵנִי וְיִתְמְכֵנִי בְּבוֹא
הַוָּלֶד עֲדֵי מַשְׁבֵּר. וְיִתֵּן בִּי כֹחַ לָלֶדֶת אֹתוֹ. אָנָּא יְיָ
סְעָדֵנִי וְאַנְשֵׁעָה וּמִצָּרוֹת תִּצְּרֵנִי בְּאוֹפָן שֶׁיֵּצֵא הַוָּלֶד
מִמֶּנִּי לְחַיִּים וְלִרְוָחָה וְלֹא יִהְיֶה בּוֹ וְלֹא בְּאֶחָד
מֵאֵבָרָיו לֹא נֶזֶק וְלֹא חִסָּרוֹן וְלֹא פֶּגַע וְלֹא מִקְרֶה וְלֹא
כְּאֵב וְלֹא צִיר וְלֹא נֶגַע וְלֹא מַחֲלָה וְהָכֵן לִי חָלָב
בְּדַדַּי מַסְפִּיק לְהָנִיק אֹתוֹ וְחָנֵּנִי שֶׁאוּכַל לְגַדְּלוֹ

(continued)

a gift, a healthy child is an answer to the
woman's prayers and a commitment to
the future. As a messenger, the child
comes endowed by God with certain
traits, bearing blessings and sometimes
hardships, all according to God's will.
Here, the petitioner asks God to send her
a child accompanied by blessings of vigor
and prosperity, for the benefit of the child
and the whole family.

husband's estate also prosper. May the wisdom of Torah abound in our community. Give us length of days, years of life that are full of love, peace, and happiness, so we may be able to love You. Spare us from the Evil Eye, from demons and from devilish spirits, from all sorrow and sadness. For You, God, are our protector and savior, now and forevermore. Listen, O Lord, I am calling to You. Be gracious unto me and answer me. Hear me, be gracious unto me, be my protector. God, listen to my plea. God, accept my prayer. Do this for Your name's sake, for the sake of Your Torah, for the sake of Your holiness. May the words of my mouth and the meditations of my heart be acceptable unto You.

Conclusion of this prayer

לְיִרְאָתֶךָ וְלַעֲבוֹדָתֶךָ. וְתִשְׁלַח בְּרָכָה רְוָחָה וְהַצְלָחָה
עִמּוֹ שֶׁיִּהְיֶה לְאִישׁ מַצְלִיחַ וְיִתְבָּרְכוּ בַּעֲבוּרוֹ גַּם נִכְסֵי
בַעְלִי. וְהַרְבֵּה גְבוּלֵנוּ בְּתַלְמוּד תּוֹרָה וְתֵן לָנוּ אֲרִיכוּת
יָמִים וּשְׁנוֹת חַיִּים בְּאַהֲבָה וּבְאַחְוָה וּבְשָׁלוֹם לְאַהֲבָה
אֶת־שֵׁם קָדְשֶׁךָ. וְתִשְׁמְרֵנוּ מֵעֵין הָרַע וּמִשֵּׁדִין
וּמִמַּזִּיקִין וּמִכָּל־צָרָה וְצוּקָה. כִּי אֵל שׁוֹמְרֵנוּ וּמַצִּילֵנוּ
אַתָּה מֵעַתָּה וְעַד עוֹלָם: שְׁמַע יְיָ קוֹלִי אֶקְרָא חָנֵּנִי
וַעֲנֵנִי: שְׁמַע יְיָ וְחָנֵּנִי יְיָ הֱיֵה עוֹזֵר לִי: שָׁמַע יְיָ תְּחִנָּתִי
יְיָ תְּפִלָּתִי יִקָּח: עֲשֵׂה לְמַעַן שְׁמֶךָ: עֲשֵׂה לְמַעַן יְמִינֶךָ:
עֲשֵׂה לְמַעַן תּוֹרָתֶךָ: עֲשֵׂה לְמַעַן קְדֻשָּׁתֶךָ: יִהְיוּ לְרָצוֹן
אִמְרֵי־פִי וְהֶגְיוֹן לִבִּי לְפָנֶיךָ יְיָ צוּרִי וְגוֹאֲלִי:

Fine de questa Orazione

Prayers to Be Said at the Onset of Labor

When a woman arrives at the hour of childbirth, she should voluntarily recite the confessional prayer, for this will make the labor easier, as it says, "You forgive all my transgressions; You heal my every disability." She should then have someone release her from her vows and then say with fervor the following psalm three times:

A PSALM of David

May the LORD answer you in time of trouble,
may the God of Jacob be your strength.
May He send you help from His sanctuary,
sustaining you from Zion.
May He remember all your offerings
and accept your sacrifices,
granting your heart's desires,
fulfilling all your hopes.

We shall sing of Your victory,
we shall acclaim the glory of our God.
May the Lord fulfill all that you ask.
Now I know that the LORD delivers His anointed.
He will answer from His heavenly abode,
bringing victory with mighty deeds.
Some trust in chariots, others in horses,
but we honor the name of the Lord our God.
They stumble and fall, but we rise and stand firm.
O LORD, deliver us! Answer us, O King, when we call.

Psalm 20

The time has come. Now is the time of trouble as revealed in the psalm. The petitioner calls on God to come to her aid now. All the transgressions she may have committed, all the mistakes she may have made have been confessed. She approaches God as pure and as worthy as a human being can be. Surely God will respond, and all those around her will sing of God's goodness.

Giunta che sia la Donna all'ora del Partorire,
sara cosa ben fatta che si disponga volontariamente
a dire il וידוי , che cio' le facilitera' il Parto,
giusta il פסוק: הסולח לכל עונכי הרפא לכל תחלואיכי
e si fara fare התרת נדרים וקללות ,
e poi dirà—con כונה il seguente מזמור tre volte

לַמְנַצֵּחַ מִזְמוֹר לְדָוִד: יַעַנְךָ יְיָ בְּיוֹם צָרָה יְשַׂגֶּבְךָ
שֵׁם ׀ אֱלֹהֵי יַעֲקֹב: יִשְׁלַח־עֶזְרְךָ מִקֹּדֶשׁ וּמִצִּיּוֹן
יִסְעָדֶךָ: יִזְכֹּר כָּל־מִנְחֹתֶיךָ וְעוֹלָתְךָ יְדַשְּׁנֶה סֶלָה: יִתֶּן־
לְךָ כִלְבָבֶךָ וְכָל־עֲצָתְךָ יְמַלֵּא: נְרַנְּנָה ׀ בִּישׁוּעָתֶךָ
וּבְשֵׁם־אֱלֹהֵינוּ נִדְגֹּל יְמַלֵּא יְיָ כָּל־מִשְׁאֲלוֹתֶיךָ: עַתָּה
יָדַעְתִּי כִּי הוֹשִׁיעַ ׀ יְיָ מְשִׁיחוֹ יַעֲנֵהוּ מִשְּׁמֵי קָדְשׁוֹ
בִּגְבוּרוֹת יֵשַׁע יְמִינוֹ: אֵלֶּה בָרֶכֶב וְאֵלֶּה בַסּוּסִים
וַאֲנַחְנוּ בְּשֵׁם־יְיָ אֱלֹהֵינוּ נַזְכִּיר: הֵמָּה כָּרְעוּ וְנָפָלוּ
וַאֲנַחְנוּ קַּמְנוּ וַנִּתְעוֹדָד: יְיָ הוֹשִׁיעָה הַמֶּלֶךְ יַעֲנֵנוּ בְיוֹם־
קָרְאֵנוּ:

Truly the might of God is greater than the strength of all the armies in the world, for what aid can horses and chariots provide her when she is in the throes of labor? And even though she is now fallen, lying upon the birthing bed, she will be saved with all Israel and again rise and stand firm.

And then she says:

ANSWER ME, God of Abraham, answer me. Answer me, Pahad Yitzhak, answer me. Answer me, Almighty One of Jacob, answer me. Answer me, Lord of mercy and forgiveness, answer me. Answer me, You who respond to those gripped in the throes of labor, answer me. Answer me, You who reclaim life from the grave and who revive the dead, answer me. Answer me, You who remember the pain of the barren woman and who open the chamber of life, answer me.

As the moment of birth approaches, as the labor advances, as the child presses to be born, the woman, in compelling litany, calls to God to help her, invoking appropriately not the distant and universal divine appellations but the personal, familial, and ancestral names of the Lord (Genesis 31:42 and 49:24).

E poi dira

עֲנֵנִי אֱלֹקֵי אַבְרָהָם עֲנֵנִי: עֲנֵנִי וּפַחַד יִצְחָק עֲנֵנִי:
עֲנֵנִי אֲבִיר יַעֲקֹב עֲנֵנִי: עֲנֵנִי אֲדוֹן הָרַחֲמִים וְהַסְּלִיחוֹת
עֲנֵנִי: עֲנֵנִי הָעוֹנֶה עֲלֵי־מַשְׁבֵּר לַחֲלוֹת עֲנֵנִי: עֲנֵנִי
הַפּוֹדֶה מִשַּׁחַת וּמְחַיֶּה מֵתִים עֲנֵנִי: עֲנֵנִי פּוֹקֵד עֲקָרוֹת
וּפוֹטֵר רֶחֶם עֲנֵנִי:

The pain referred to here is both the pain of the struggles of a laboring woman and the anguish of a woman with empty arms who desperately desires a child. In both cases, God has the power to remove the pain and be gracious.

MAY THE EXALTED, mighty, and awesome God, who in times of trouble answers those who fear Him, accept my prayer and the pleas of His entire people, the House of Israel. And amidst their company, may He remember and tenderly care for a woman, bound up and struggling as if bearing her first child. From within this struggle, through her pains and labor, her heart trembles and calls out. So it is with me today as I sit upon the birthing stool. My gaze is fixed upon the Lord, my God. May He see my pain and my tears, and grant my petition. May my prayer be welcome. God in His mercy will deliver me. God in His compassion will release me. He will return my health and vigor and well-being. He will restore my former strength. My body will once again be refreshed.

(continued)

God is depicted here as midwife, attending to the delivery, holding the gaze of the woman in labor, focusing her attention, coaching her through the intensifying waves of pain.

The last line of this petition was re-

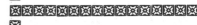

הָאֵל הַגָּדוֹל הַגִּבּוֹר וְהַנּוֹרָא הָעוֹנֶה לְעִתּוֹת בַּצָּרָה
אֶת־יְרֵאָיו הוּא יְקַבֵּל תְּפִלָּתִי וּתְפִלּוֹת כָּל־עַמּוֹ בֵּית־
יִשְׂרָאֵל. וּבְכֻלָּם יִזְכּוֹר וְיִפְקוֹד לְטוֹבָה וּלְרַחֲמִים
לְאִשָּׁה עֲצוּרָה וְצָרָה כְּמַבְכִּירָה וְלִבָּהּ מִצָּרָה תָּחִיל
תִּזְעַק כַּחֲבָלֶיהָ וְצִירֶיהָ כְּאָנֹכִי הַיּוֹם הַיּוֹשֶׁבֶת עַל־
הַמַּשְׁבֵּר־שִׁבְרִי עַל־יְיָ אֱלֹהַי הוּא יִרְאֶה בְּצָרָתִי
וְדִמְעָתִי וְיֵעָתֵר לַעֲתִירָתִי. וְיַעֲלֶה לְרָצוֹן תְּפִלָּתִי. הוּא
בְּרַחֲמָיו הָרַבִּים יְפַלְּטֵנִי. הוּא כַּחֲסָדָיו הָרַבִּים יְחַלְּצֵנִי.
עַל כֵּן כָּן הַבְּרִיאוּת וְהַחַיִּים וְהַשָּׁלוֹם יוֹשִׁיבֵנִי. וּלְאֵיתָנִי
הָרִאשׁוֹן יָשִׁיבֵנִי. *רְפָאוֹת תִּחְיֶה לִשְׁרִי וְשִׁקּוּי*
לְעַצְמוֹתָי.

(continued)

cited on behalf of Miriam, Moses' sister.
This five-word poetic prayer is the short-
est in the entire Bible. And by creative

transference the petitioner is encouraged
to believed Moses is also reciting it on her
behalf.

95

The most Majestic One, the one who heard and answered the prayers of our holy and pure matriarchs, who by nature were barren, He undid their barrenness and reversed their condition. He cared for them with graciousness as deep and as wide as the sea. God remembered them and blessed them with children.

So may He remember and tend to me now, at this moment, with goodness and mercy and kindness and tenderness, as I pray before Him. He will relieve my pain and my distress. He will not intensify my suffering.

For my eyes are fixed on Him alone, even as a handmaid attends closely to her mistress, until He delivers me into ease and comfort.

"Arise, shine for Your light has dawned; the glory of the Lord has shone upon you" (Isaiah 60:1). And it is written, "Moses cried to the Lord, saying 'Please, God, please, heal her'" (Numbers 12:13).

Then say the following verse three times:

THEN ALL these courtiers of yours shall come down to me and bow low to me, saying, "Depart, you and all the people who follow you! And after that I will depart," and he left.

And he left. I will depart and after that who follow you, people all the and you depart saying to me low bow and down to me come shall these courtiers of yours, then all (Exodus 11:8).

Once again the woman is directed to recite a biblical phrase in a mantric tone.

This verse packs together in dramatic form the central thought occupying the

מֶלֶךְ מַלְכֵי הַמְּלָכִים שֶׁשָּׁמַע וְעָנָה תְּפִלּוֹת הָאִמָּהוֹת הַקְּדוֹשׁוֹת וְהַטְּהוֹרוֹת שֶׁהָיוּ בְּטִבְעָן עֲקָרוֹת וְהָפַךְ וְשִׁנָּה מַעֲרַכְתָּן לְטוֹבָה. וְהִשְׁגִּיחַ עֲלֵיהֶן בְּמִדַּת הָרַחֲמִים מִנִּי יָם אֲרֻכָּה וּרְחָבָה וְהָיוּ מֵאִתּוֹ נִפְקָדוֹת וְנִזְכָּרוֹת בְּזֶרַע אֲנָשִׁים. הוּא יִפְקוֹד וְיִזְכּוֹר לְטוֹבָה לְחֵן וּלְחֶסֶד וּלְרַחֲמִים אוֹתִי בָּעֵת וּבָעוֹנָה הַזֹּאת אֲשֶׁר אָנֹכִי מִתְפַּלֶּלֶת לְפָנָיו. וְהוּא יָנִיחֵנִי מִמַּחֲלִי וְעָצְבִּי וְלֹא יוֹסִיף לְדַאֲבֵנִי. כִּי עֵינַי תְּלֻיּוֹת אֵלָיו לְבַדּוֹ כְּשִׁפְחָה אֶל יַד גְּבִרְתָּהּ עַד שֶׁיּוֹצִיא אוֹתִי לִרְוָחָה אָמֵן: קוּמִי אוֹרִי כִּי בָא אוֹרֵךְ וּכְבוֹד יְיָ עָלַיִךְ זָרָח: וְנֶאֱמַר וַיִּצְעַק מֹשֶׁה אֶל יְיָ לֵאמֹר אֵל נָא רְפָא נָא לָהּ:

E poi dirà tre volte che segue

וַיֵּרְדוּ כָל־עֲבָדֶיךָ אֵלֶּה אֵלַי וְהִשְׁתַּחֲווּ לִי לֵאמֹר צֵא אַתָּה וְכָל־הָעָם אֲשֶׁר בְּרַגְלֶיךָ וְאַחֲרֵי כֵן אֵצֵא וַיֵּצֵא: וַיֵּצֵא אֵצֵא כֵן וְאַחֲרֵי בְּרַגְלֶיךָ אֲשֶׁר הָעָם וְכָל אַתָּה צֵא לֵאמֹר לִי וְהִשְׁתַּחֲווּ אֵלַי אֵלֶּה עֲבָדֶיךָ כָל וַיֵּרְדוּ:

laboring woman: get the baby out. Earlier (see p. 87) the verse was recited in anticipation of labor. Now the moment has come.

And then she says:

"**NO** woman in your land shall miscarry or be barren. I will let You enjoy the full count of your days" (Exodus 23:26). Most Majestic One, let the light of Your tenderness shine upon me, as it is written, "Arise and shine, for Your light has dawned. The presence of the Lord has shone upon you" (Isaiah 60:1).

"You decree and it will be fulfilled. And light will shine upon your affairs" (Job 22:28).

May the Most Majestic One annul all harsh and harmful decrees, and may He relieve me of all my agony and all my afflictions. May He forgive all my sins and renew my youth like the eagle's, as it is written, "In fleeting anger, for a moment, I hid my face from You, but with kindness everlasting I will take you back in love, said the Lord your Redeemer" (Isaiah 54:8).

May the Most Majestic One in his abundant graciousness open the gates of light for me. Amen.

The Lord of Hosts is with us; the God of Jacob is our haven.

Lord of Hosts, happy is one who relies upon You.

Lord grant victory. May the King answer us when we call. May the words of my mouth and the meditations of my heart be acceptable to You, my Rock and my Redeemer.

Conclusion

Darkness and labor. Light and delivery.

For the laboring woman, the world around her turns dark and falls away. All her energies are turned inward, concentrating on bringing the baby safely out of her womb and into the world. Sight beyond the birthing bed is limited. Darkness is all around. Yet, with delivery, her focus widens. Her eyes are open, her vision is restored, the light rushes back. She searches and reaches for the child she has just brought forth.

E poi dira

לֹא תִהְיֶה מְשַׁכֵּלָה וַעֲקָרָה בְּאַרְצֶךָ אֶת־מִסְפַּר יָמֶיךָ
אֲמַלֵּא׃ מֶלֶךְ מַלְכֵי הַמְּלָכִים בְּרַחֲמָיו יָאִיר בְּחֶמְלָתוֹ
עָלַי׃ כַּכָּתוּב קוּמִי אוֹרִי כִּי בָא אוֹרֵךְ וּכְבוֹד יְיָ עָלַיִךְ
זָרָח׃ וְתִגְזַר אֹמֶר וְיָקֶם לָךְ וְעַל דְּרָכַיִךְ נָגַהּ אוֹר׃ מֶלֶךְ
מַלְכֵי הַמְּלָכִים יְבַטֵּל מִמֶּנִּי כָּל־גְּזֵרוֹת קָשׁוֹת וְרָעוֹת׃
וְיִרְפָּאֵנִי מִכָּל־מַכְאוֹבַי וּמַכּוֹתַי׃ וִיכַפֵּר אֶת־חַטֹּאתַי׃
וִיחַדֵּשׁ כִּנְשֶׁר נְעוּרָי׃ כַּכָּתוּב בְּשֶׁצֶף קֶצֶף הִסְתַּרְתִּי
פָנַי רֶגַע מִמֵּךְ וּבְחֶסֶד עוֹלָם רִחַמְתִּיךְ אָמַר גֹּאֲלֵךְ יְיָ׃
מֶלֶךְ מַלְכֵי הַמְּלָכִים בְּרַחֲמָיו יִפְתַּח לִי שַׁעֲרֵי אוֹרָה
אָמֵן׃ יְיָ צְבָאוֹת עִמָּנוּ מִשְׂגָּב לָנוּ אֱלֹקֵי יַעֲקֹב סֶלָה׃ יְיָ
צְבָאוֹת אַשְׁרֵי אָדָם בֹּטֵחַ בָּךְ׃ יְיָ הוֹשִׁיעָה הַמֶּלֶךְ
יַעֲנֵנוּ בְיוֹם קָרְאֵנוּ׃ יִהְיוּ לְרָצוֹן אִמְרֵי פִי וְהֶגְיוֹן לִבִּי
לְפָנֶיךָ יְיָ צוּרִי וְגֹאֲלִי׃

Fine

Light in this prayer symbolizes God's mercy, goodness, and forgiveness. The prayer opens with a promise to be fulfilled only if the Israelites obey all God's commands and serve Him faithfully. But who can be completely obedient? Who can be sure their fidelity is constant? So the woman invokes not her merit but God's forgiveness, and God's love, to see her through.

Here is another prayer to be recited at the hour of childbirth:

LORD of Hosts, please attend to the pain of Your maidservant. Remember me. Do not forget Your humble servant. Give Your devoted one a child. God of Israel, grant me my desire. Like a deer yearns for the flowing waters in the hour that she comes to give birth; as her labor gets harder, she reaches for You with her antlers. Bitterly she invokes your mercy, for in Your hands You hold the keys to life. You are merciful and open her womb, tenderly and warmly. So does my soul cry for You, God, and request Your mercy and goodness.

Open the wall of my womb so that I may at the proper time bear this child who is within me—at a time of blessing and salvation. May the child be vital and healthy. May I not struggle only to achieve emptiness, may I not labor in vain, God forbid. Because You alone hold the key to life, as it is written, "And God remembered Rachel and listened to her and opened her womb" (Genesis 30:22).

Therefore, take pity on my entreaty. From the very depths of my heart I call to You. I raise my voice to You, God. Answer me from the heights of Your holiness. Selah.

(continued)

Labor often seems endless, especially if there is no perceived or steady progress. Amidst this wilderness of pain and fear, the woman searches for salvation. As natural as it is for a deer to seek the rushing water in her hour of need, the prayer says, so is it natural for women to turn to God.

The fourth paragraph of the prayer is largely written in Aramaic (see italicized section of the prayer), most unusual for this book. Indeed, the first phrase of the

Altra תפלה da celebrarsi nell'ora del Parto

אָנָּא יְיָ צְבָאוֹת רָאֹה תִרְאֶה בָּעֳנִי אֲמָתֶךְ וּזְכַרְתָּנִי
וְלֹא תִשְׁכַּח אֶת־אֲמָתֶךְ וְנָתַתָּ לַאֲמָתֶךְ זֶרַע אֲנָשִׁים.
וֵאלֹהֵי יִשְׂרָאֵל יִתֵּן אֶת־שְׁאֵלָתִי. וּכְאַיָּל תַּעֲרוֹג עַל
אֲפִיקֵי מַיִם בְּשָׁעָה שֶׁמְבַקֶּשֶׁת לָלֶדֶת וּמִתְקַשִּׁין עָלֶיהָ
צִירֶיהָ עוֹרֶגֶת לָךְ בְּקַרְנֶיהָ וְצוֹעֶקֶת בְּקוֹל מַר עַל
רַחֲמֶיךָ. כִּי בְּיָדְךָ מַפְתֵּחַ שֶׁל חַיָּה וְאַתָּה מְרַחֵם
וּפוֹתֵחַ אֶת רַחְמָהּ בְּחֶסֶד וּבְרַחֲמִים. כֵּן נַפְשִׁי תַּעֲרוֹג
אֵלֶיךָ אֱלֹקִים וּמְבַקֶּשֶׁת רַחֲמֶיךָ וַחֲסָדֶיךָ לִפְתּוֹחַ פֶּתַח
צִירֵי רַחֲמֵי לָלֶדֶת הַוָּלָד אֲשֶׁר בְּקִרְבִּי בְּשָׁעָה רְאוּיָה
לָלֶדֶת בְּעֵת בְּרָכָה וִישׁוּעָה. בְּוָלָד שֶׁל קַיָמָא שֶׁלֹא
אִיגַע עַצְמִי לָרִיק וְלֹא אֵלֵד לַבֶּהָלָה חַס וְשָׁלוֹם. כִּי
בְּיָדְךָ לְבַד מַפְתֵּחַ שֶׁל חַיָּה. כְּדִכְתִיב וַיִּזְכֹּר אֱלֹקִים
אֶת רָחֵל וַיִּשְׁמַע אֵלֶיהָ אֱלֹקִים וַיִּפְתַּח אֶת־רַחְמָהּ. עַל
כֵּן יִכְמְרוּ רַחֲמֶיךָ אֶל־תַּחֲנוּנַי וּמִמַּעֲמַקֵּי הַלֵּב
קְרָאתִיךָ יְיָ. קוֹלִי אֵלֶיךָ אֶקְרָא וְתַעֲנֵנִי מֵהַר קָדְשֶׁךָ
סֶלָה.

(continued)

Aramaic is preceded by a Hebrew translation, allowing the conclusion that the Aramaic segment was drawn as a unit from an earlier traditional source.

Whatever the source, it depicts a courtroom scene in which the Other Side,

the force that argues for death, tries to take advantage of woman's vulnerability. It brings a case against her when she is least able to defend herself. At such a moment, the *yetadot* speak for the

(continued)

Listen, God, to my prayer. Let my plea come before You, for I call to You with a full heart, with enduring love and total devotion. May the angels called *yetadot* who are assigned to attend to the labor of women, those *angels appointed to tend to the labor of the womb, who are called* yetadot, *gather up the cries of women and place them before the Holy Throne. And when the Other Side comes to make charges, cleverly choosing this moment of vulnerability, let the angels come forward and bring the cries to the guardian of the heavenly portal. Then the Other Side will not be able to speak against me.* So may my prayer come before You, for You have commanded us to be fruitful and multiply, and to raise our children in the ways of Torah and *mitzvot*, to stand before You and serve You and to bless Your holy name. Do not allow the Other Side any opportunities to argue against me or against the child within me. Remember me for good. Do not forget Your maidservant. Give Your devoted one a holy, healthy child. The Lord of Hosts is with us. The God of Jacob is our fortress. Selah. Lord of Hosts, happy is the one who trusts in You. Help us, Lord. Answer us, O King, when we call.

May the words of my mouth and the meditations of my heart be acceptable to You, my Rock and my Redeemer.

Conclusion of the preceding prayer

woman, bringing as evidence the woman's own voice.

Literally, *yetadot* means *pegs*. They mark the circumference, guard the boundaries, secure the structure of the domain they define. No one can gain entrance without passing between them. They are the infrastructure that supports the whole. Literally, the mention of pegs recalls the story of Yael in the Book of Judges (Chapter 4). The Israelites were fighting against the Canaanite army, whose commander was Sisera. The Israelite army, led by Deborah, routed Sisera, who fled in retreat to what he believed was friendly territory and hid in the tent of Heber the Kerite, who was Yael's husband. Yael welcomed Sisera, feigning protection. In truth, Sisera was not safe, for as he slept, Yael took a mallet and drove a tent peg through Sisera's temple.

The peg conjures up images of life and justified death. Its appearance here can be understood as follows:

Traditional belief holds that no act on earth occurs without God's knowledge and without God's consent. Hence, all deaths must be justified. Death in childbirth was all too common and all too confounding. Here is an attempt to explain rationally and justly its occurrence and its frequency, for, on occasion, the other side might just win.

Interestingly, the woman says, "You

הַאֲזִינָה יְיָ תְּפִלָּתִי וְשַׁוְעָתִי אֵלֶיךָ תָבֹא אֲשֶׁר
אֲנִי צוֹעֶקֶת לְפָנֶיךָ בְּלֶב־שָׁלֵם בִּרְעוּת וּבְאַהֲבָה רַבָּה.
וּמַלְאֲכֵי מַעְלָה הַמְמֻנִּים עַל הַמַּשְׁבֵּר הַנִּקְרָאִים
יְתֵדוֹת. חֲיָלִין מְמַנָּן עַל הַמַּשְׁבֵּר דְּאִקְרוּן בִּשְׁמַיְהוּ
יְתֵדוֹת דְּנַטְלֵי אִנּוּן קָלֵי דְּנָשִׁין וּמְנַחָן לְהוֹן קָמֵיהּ
הַהוּא הֵכְלָא. וְכַד הַהוּא סִטְרָא אַחֲרָא אָתֵי לְקַטְרְגָא
בְּהַאי שַׁעְתָּא דְּאִיהִי שַׁעְתָּא דְּסַכָּנָה קַיְּמֵי אִלֵּין
וּמֵעָלִין הָנֵי קָלֵי לַמְמַנָּא דְּעַל פִּתְחָא וְלָא יָכִיל הַהוּא
סִטְרָא אַחֲרָא לְקַטְרְגָא. בֵּן תְּפִלָּתִי אֵלֶיךָ תָבֹא אֲשֶׁר
צִוִּיתָ אֵלֵינוּ לִפְרוֹת וְלִרְבּוֹת וּלְגַדֵּל בָּנִים לַתּוֹרָה
וּמִצְוֹת לַעֲמוֹד לְפָנֶיךָ וּלְשָׁרְתֶךָ וּלְבָרֵךְ בִּשְׁמֶךָ. וְאַל
תִּתֵּן מָקוֹם לַסִּטְרָא אַחֲרָא לְקַטְרֵג עָלַי אוֹ עַל פְּרִי
בִטְנִי וּזְכַרְתָּנִי לְטוֹבָה וְלֹא תִשְׁכַּח אֶת אֲמָתֶךָ וְנָתַתָּה
לַאֲמָתֶךָ זֶרַע קֹדֶשׁ שֶׁל קַיָּמָא: יְיָ צְבָאוֹת עִמָּנוּ מִשְׂגָּב
לָנוּ אֱלֹקֵי יַעֲקֹב סֶלָה: יְיָ צְבָאוֹת אַשְׁרֵי אָדָם בֹּטֵחַ
בָּךְ: יְיָ הוֹשִׁיעָה הַמֶּלֶךְ יַעֲנֵנוּ בְיוֹם קָרְאֵנוּ:

Fine della presente Orazione

have commanded us to be fruitful and multiply." This commandment was given only to men, it being argued that child-birth is life-threatening and one cannot be commanded to do that which threatens one's existence. Yet, here the woman phrases the commandment as if it were meant for her as well. How clever! For surely God would not permit her to die in the performance of a commandment.

Prayers to Be Said at the Beginning of Delivery

This prayer should be said at the onset of delivery:

LORD, God of Hosts Who sits amid the cherubs and who judges the righteous with integrity, You have tried us and punished us since the creation of the world and humanity, stipulating that we women shall give birth to our children in pain, as it is written in Your Torah, "In pain shall you bear children" (Genesis 3:16). But everything is within Your power, everything within Your hands. Those to whom You show kindness are relieved. Those to whom You are compassionate are comforted. Who will tell You what to do, God? For the sake of Your abundant kindness, have mercy upon me. For the sake of all the righteous men and all the righteous women upon whom You have showered Your mercy, be gracious unto me. You heard the petition of women in labor and heeded their cry when they called upon You to open their wombs. And You opened them, in kindness and in mercy, and they bore children, softly, as the walls of their wombs opened. God, You were before the creation of the world. You sustained the world until now through Your abundant goodness. Surely You can remove my suffering from me. Do not approach your maidservant in judgment. Do not listen to the voices of the adversarial angels who approach You to counsel against me. Rather heed the voices of the righteous angels and those who speak the truth, who will speak for and defend Your people Israel and me. To them, listen; receive their words and their advocacy. Answer their pleas; do their bidding promptly.

(continued)

The first chapter of the Book of Samuel speaks of Hannah, the wife of Elkanah, who was barren and desperately wanted a child. She went to the local holy place (before the Temple was built) and poured her heart out before God. Her silent but compelling petition was misunderstood as drunkenness by the local priest, but it moved God so that He granted her a child. Hannah's silent prayer henceforth

Questa תפלה dee dirsi quando cominciano le Doglie

יְיָ אֱלֹהֵי הַצְּבָאוֹת יֹשֵׁב הַכְּרֻבִים שֹׁפֵט צֶדֶק בֶּאֱמוּנָה
אַתָּה הוֹכַחְתָּ וְיִסַּרְתָּ אֹתָנוּ מִבְּרִיאַת עוֹלָם וְאָדָם
שֶׁאָנוּ נָשִׁים נֵלֵד אֶת בָּנֵינוּ בְּצַעַר. כְּמוֹ שֶׁכָּתוּב
בְּתוֹרָתֶךָ בְּעֶצֶב תֵּלְדִי בָנִים. וְהַכֹּל בִּרְשׁוּתֶךָ. וּבְיָדְךָ
הַכֹּל אֶת אֲשֶׁר תָּחֹן יוּחַן וְאֶת אֲשֶׁר תְּרַחֵם יְרוּחַם
בְּאֵין מוֹחָה. וּמִי יֹאמַר לְךָ מַה תַּעֲשֶׂה. יְיָ לְמַעַן
רַחֲמֶיךָ הָרַבִּים רַחֵם עָלַי לְמַעַן זְכוּת כָּל־הַצַּדִּיקִים
וּבִזְכוּת כָּל־הַנָּשִׁים הַצִּדְקָנִיּוֹת שֶׁאַתָּה מְרַחֵם עֲלֵיהֶן
וְשָׁמַעְתָּ וְהַאֲזַנְתָּ לְקוֹל צַעֲקָתָן בְּעֵת שַׁוְּעָן אֵלֶיךָ
שֶׁתִּפְתַּח אֶת רַחֲמָן וּפָתַחְתָּ אֹתָן בְּחֶסֶד וּבְרַחֲמִים
וְיָלְדוּ בְּחֶסֶד וְצִירֵי דַלְתֵי בִטְנָן נִפְתָּחוּ: יְיָ אַתָּה הָיִיתָ
קֹדֶם בְּרִיאַת עוֹלָם וְאַתָּה נָשָׂאתָ אֶת הָעוֹלָם עֲדֵי עַד.
בְּחַסְדְּךָ הַגָּדוֹל הָסֵר עֳנִי מִמֶּנִּי. וְאַל תָּבֹא בְמִשְׁפָּט
אֶת־אֲמָתֶךָ.

(continued)

---

served as the model for the *Sh'moneh Esrai*,
the central silent prayer of every service.

Tears possess a special, divine currency.
Tears of pain, of sorrow, of contrition can
gain access to the Lord even when prayers

cannot. "Even when the gates of prayer
are closed, the gates of tears remain open"
(*Berakhot* 32b).

Keep them forever before You to serve as our advocates of truth and merit. Take the key of pregnancy in Your right hand and unlock my belly without pain or suffering, without harm or deformity. Weaken the grip of the Evil Impulse upon the son or daughter who is within me, and strengthen within him or her the impulse for good. Protect me and my child, whatever it might be, male or female, from all evil spirits, from all dread disease, and may the Evil Eye have no dominion over us. God, Lord of Hosts, listen and heed my cries of need. Place my tears within Your special pouch, within Your treasure house. Accept me the way You accepted the prayers and tears of Hannah, about whom You caused Eli the Kohen to prophesy that her prayers would soon come true. For this is what he said to her, "Go in peace. The God of Israel will give you that which you asked of Him" (I Samuel 1:17). For You, God, for Your own sake, readily welcome the prayers of those who call to You, in truth and purity. May the words of my mouth and the meditations of my heart be acceptable to You, Lord, my Rock and my Redeemer.

Conclusion

וְאַל תַּאֲזִין לְקוֹל הַמַּלְאָכִים הַמְקַטְרְגִים
לְפָנֶיךָ כְּנֶגְדִּי לִפְנֵי כִּסֵּא כְבוֹדֶךָ. וּלְמַלְאֲכֵי צֶדֶק
וּמְלִיצֵי יוֹשֶׁר אֲשֶׁר הֵם מְלַמְּדִים וּמְלִיצִים סַנֵּגוֹרְיָא
וּזְכוּת עַל עַמְּךָ בֵּית יִשְׂרָאֵל וְעָלַי אֲלֵיהֶם תַּטֶּה אָזְנֶךָ
וְתִשְׁמַע וּתְקַבֵּל דִּבְרֵיהֶם וְסַנֵּגוֹרְיָא שֶׁלָּהֶם. וַעֲנֵה אֶת
עֲתִירָתָם וַעֲשֵׂה מִיָּד בַּקָּשָׁתָם. וְהַעֲמִידֵם תָּמִיד
לְפָנֶיךָ לִהְיוֹת לָנוּ לִמְלִיצֵי יוֹשֶׁר וּזְכוּת. וְקַח אֶת
הַמַּפְתֵּחַ שֶׁל הֵרָיוֹן בְּיַד יְמִינֶךָ וּפְתַח הֵרְיוֹנִי בְּלִי עֶצֶב
וְצַעַר בְּלִי גֶזֶק וּבְלִי חִסָּרוֹן. וְחַלֵּשׁ מֵהַוָּלֵד אוֹ הַיַּלְדָּה
אֲשֶׁר בְּמֵעַי אֶת־הַיֵּצֶר הָרָע וְחַזְּק־בּוֹ אֶת הַיֵּצֶר
הַטּוֹב. וּשְׁמוֹר אוֹתִי וְאֶת הַוָּלֵד יִהְיֶה מַה־שֶׁיִּהְיֶה אִם
זָכָר אוֹ נְקֵבָה מִכָּל־רוּחוֹת רָעוֹת וּמִכָּל־מַרְעִין בִּישִׁין
וְאַל יִשְׁלוֹט בָּנוּ עַיִן הָרָע: יְיָ אֱלֹקֵי הַצְּבָאוֹת תִּשְׁמַע
וְתַאֲזִין לְקוֹל שַׁוְעָתִי וְשִׂימָה דִמְעָתִי בְּנֹאדֶךָ
בְּאוֹצְרוֹתֶךָ. וּתְקַבְּלֵנִי כְּמוֹ שֶׁקִּבַּלְתָּ הַתְּפִלָּה וְהַדִּמְעָה
שֶׁל חַנָּה שֶׁהִשְׁרֵת נְבוּאָה עַל עֵלִי הַכֹּהֵן וּבִשַּׁרְתָּ אֹתָהּ
עַל יָדוֹ. שֶׁכָּךְ אָמַר לָהּ לְכִי לְשָׁלוֹם וֵאלֹקֵי יִשְׂרָאֵל
יִתֵּן אֶת שֵׁלָתֵךְ אֲשֶׁר שָׁאַלְתְּ מֵעִמּוֹ. כִּי אַתָּה לְמַעַן
רַחֲמֶיךָ מוּכָן לְקַבֵּל תְּפִלַּת הַקּוֹרְאִים אֵלֶיךָ בְּכָל
לְבָבָם: יִהְיוּ לְרָצוֹן אִמְרֵי פִי וְהֶגְיוֹן לִבִּי לְפָנֶיךָ יְיָ צוּרִי
וְגוֹאֲלִי:

Fine

Prayer to Be Said after Safely Giving Birth

This prayer is to be said by a woman after she has safely given birth:

MAY IT BE Your will, Lord my God and God of my forebears, King of Mercy, who acts with grace and compassion, that just as You saved me from the profound strains of childbirth and from its awesome dangers, so may Your compassion be stirred to save all women from such dangers, all daughters of Abraham, Isaac, and Jacob, Your beloved seed. And just as You have saved me this time, so may You show me the same sign of Your favor each time I give birth. May the words of my mouth and the meditations of my heart be acceptable to You, God, my Rock and my Redeemer.

Conclusion

The sole attribute of God referred to in this prayer is compassion. Mentioned three times, it is represented in the Hebrew by the root רחם . In a tender relationship of terms, רחם is also the Hebrew word for *womb*.

In opening the walls of the womb, the prayer seems to tell us, God opens the gates of divine mercy, and through this act of extending divine benevolence to humankind, God makes room for life. Justice, righteousness, and truth alone cannot sustain the world. Sometimes, the world needs the gift of divine compassion.

Questa תפלה dee dirsi dalla Donna dopo di avere felicemente partorito

יְהִי רָצוֹן מִלְּפָנֶיךָ יְיָ אֱלֹקַי וֵאלֹקֵי אֲבוֹתַי מֶלֶךְ רַחְמָן
וּמְרַחֵם שֶׁכְּשֵׁם שֶׁהִצַּלְתַּנִי מֵהַצָּרָה הַגְּדוֹלָה הַזֹּאת וּמִן
הַסַּכָּנָה הָעֲצוּמָה זֹאת כַּךְ יִכָּמְרוּ רַחֲמֶיךָ לְהַצִּיל מִן
הַסַּכָּנָה זֹאת לְכָל־בְּנוֹת אַבְרָהָם יִצְחָק וְיַעֲקֹב זֶרַע
אֲהוּבֶךָ. וּכְשֵׁם שֶׁהִצַּלְתַּנִי עַתָּה כַּךְ עֲשֵׂה עִמִּי אוֹת
לְטוֹבָה בְּכָל־פַּעַם שֶׁאֶלֵד: יִהְיוּ לְרָצוֹן אִמְרֵי־פִי
וְהֶגְיוֹן לִבִּי לְפָנֶיךָ יְיָ צוּרִי וְגוֹאֲלִי:

Fine

Humanity's needs are as boundless as God's mercies. No sooner is one prayer answered than another replaces it before the throne of divine mercy. So too here. Before relinquishing her divine audience, the new mother offers one more prayer. Even as God graciously responded to this woman, this time, so is God asked to respond always to all women, including the petitioner. It takes great strength to speak of the next time amid the soiled linens and fresh memories of childbirth.

Prayer to Be Said When She Nurses for the First Time

This prayer is to be said by a woman the first time she nurses her infant:

MAY IT BE Your will, Lord my God and God of my forebears, that you provide nourishment for your humble creation, this tiny child, plenty of milk, as much as he needs.

Give me the disposition and inclination to find the time to nurse him patiently until he be satisfied.

Cause me to sleep lightly so that the moment he cries I will hear and respond.

Spare me the horror of accidentally smothering my child while I sleep, God forbid.

May the words of my mouth and the meditations of my heart be acceptable to You, my Rock and my Redeemer.

Some things are eternal: concern about the quantity of milk she produces, concern about the number of tasks that press upon her, concern about the sheer exhaus- tion that would prevent her from properly nourishing her child. But one concern, rarely voiced today, is the fear of smoth- ering a child. Yet, infants were often

Questa תפילה dee dirsi dalla Donna la prima
volte che porge il Latte al suo Fanciullino.

יְהִי רָצוֹן מִלְּפָנֶיךָ יְיָ אֱלֹקַי וֵאלֹקֵי אֲבוֹתַי שֶׁתַּזְמִין
מָזוֹן עַבְדְּךָ הַתִּינוֹק הַזֶּה בְּרֻבּוֹי חָלָב דֵּי מַחְסוֹרוֹ
אֲשֶׁר יֶחְסַר לוֹ. וְשִׂים בְּלִבְכִי הָעֵת שֶׁצָּרִיךְ לְהָנִיקֵהוּ
כְּדֵי לָתֵת לוֹ. וְהָקֵל מֵעָלַי הַשֵּׁנָה. וּבְעֵת שֶׁיִּבְכֶּה פְּתַח
אָזְנַי כְּדֵי לְשָׁמְעוֹ מִיָּד. וְהַצִּילֵנִי שֶׁלֹּא תִפּוֹל יָדִי עָלָיו
בְּעֵת הַשֵּׁנָה וְיָמוּת חַס וְשָׁלוֹם: יִהְיוּ לְרָצוֹן אִמְרֵי־פִי
וְהֶגְיוֹן לִבִּי לְפָנֶיךָ יְיָ צוּרִי וְגוֹאֲלִי:

taken into their parents' bed in winter to
ward off the cold. The fear expressed here
is that of rolling over and smothering the
child by lying on her. Did this indeed happen? Or did children then, as now,
sadly die of Sudden Infant Death Syn-
drome, and their mothers, unable to
fathom why, tragically blame themselves?

111

Prayer to Be Said before Her Son's Circumcision

When the mother relinquishes her tender son to be taken for the circumcision, she must realize that she is exposing him to possible death for the honor of God. She is to say over the little boy the following prayer, and she should recite it with great fervor, for at this precise moment she will be easily heard.

MAY IT BE   Your will, Lord my God and God of my forebears, that just as this newborn child is pleasing to You now, for he is without sin and without fault, so may he always be before You. Therefore, may his *brit* be without blemish. Do not lead him into temptation or shame. May he always be in good health so he may do Your bidding. May he always be God fearing. May neither his intention nor his desires be diverted from the study of Your holy Torah or from doing Your commandments. And may he be this way with You until the day he dies.

(continued)

A mother's heart is full as she gives up her newborn son to be circumcised. This precious baby, fresh from the trials of childbirth, is now to be entered into the covenant of Israel through a most ancient, dangerous ritual.

The mother knows that in every begin-ning are the seeds of every end. She asks God to protect and provide for her son his entire life. Her influence is limited; her protection fleeting. Soon her child will be on his own. If God does not provide for his needs, he will end up in debt, in service to others. But service to others

Quando la Madre contegna il suo Figliuolo per che
sia portato all מילה, dee figurarsi nella suamente
di esporlo a certe morte per onore di Dio; e dee
dire sopra il Fanciullo la seguente תפלה , e
dee dirla con grande כונה , perche in quell'ora verrà
facilmente ascoltata.

יְהִי רָצוֹן מִלְפָנֶיךָ יְיָ אֱלֹקַי וֵאלֹקֵי אֲבוֹתַי שֶׁכְּשֵׁם
שֶׁהוּא רָצוּי לְפָנֶיךָ עַכְשָׁו שֶׁאֵין בּוֹ לֹא חֵטְא וְלֹא עָוֹן
כַּךְ יִהְיֶה תָמִיד לְפָנֶיךָ שֶׁלֹא יִפְגּוֹם בְּרִיתוֹ. וְאַל
תְּבִיאֵהוּ לִידֵי נִסָּיוֹן וְלֹא לִידֵי בִזָּיוֹן. וִיהִי בָּרִיא אוֹלָם
לַעֲבוֹדָתֶךָ. וְתָמִיד יִהְיֶה נֶגֶד פָּנָיו יְרְאָתֶךָ. וְלֹא יָסִיר
דַּעְתּוֹ וּרְצוֹנוֹ מִלְמוּד תּוֹרָתֶךָ וּמֵעֲשִׂיַת מִצְוֹתֶיךָ וִיהִי

(continued)

interferes with service to God, which
requires a sense of dignity, independence,
and freedom. What is good for her child,
the petitioner argues, is good for
God—an almost irresistible petition.

And as the portal to the covenant opens
to welcome a new member, so does it
open wide the portal of prayer to God.
Thresholds—symbols and artifacts of
transition—provide special opportunities
of access along with their own measure
of vulnerability. Dangerous as this time
of circumcision is, it is also a time of
unimpeded access to God.

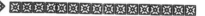

Provide him with a livelihood from Your hand, that he need not rely on any flesh-and-blood, for such dependency would serve as a barrier keeping him from serving You fully. He would be covered with shame and disgrace if forced to turn to others who are base and venal, who dispense their gifts stingily, a little here, a little there. For when we need to rely on others, our wisdom is perverted, our souls grieve, our flesh aches. But such is not the case with one who receives sustenance from Your kind, generous, outstretched, open, and bountiful hands. May my child never be beholden to others.

And should my child merit the blessings of old age, may it be Your will to spare him from all sufferings, both large and small. May sickness never befall him. May You keep him from all harm and accident so that he is always ready to do Your bidding. May You make his desires match Your desires. May he not be hindered by any stumbling blocks, neither with regard to ordained tasks nor with regard to daily needs. May he recover in full vigor from any illness and wound. May he live to see his sons and daughters happily married, dedicated to the Torah and commandments. May he not suffer a lingering or unnatural death. And may he come whole before the Holy One, blessed be He. Amen. May the words of my mouth and the meditations of my heart be acceptable to You, my Rock and my Redeemer.

בֶן עַמְּךָ עַד יוֹם מוֹתוֹ. וְתַזְמִין לוֹ פַּרְנָסָתוֹ מִיָּדֶךָ. וְאַל
תְּבִיאֵהוּ לִידֵי בָּשָׂר וָדָם שֶׁזֶּהוּ מָסַךְ מַבְדִּיל לוֹ שֶׁלֹּא
יוּכַל לְעָבְדֶךָ בִּהְיוֹתוֹ מְכֻסֶּה בוֹשֶׁת וּכְלִימָה לְצַפּוֹת
מִיַּד בָּשָׂר וָדָם נָבָל וְכַפְדָן וּמַתְּנָתוֹ מְעוּטָה וְזְעֵיר שָׁם
וְזְעֵיר שָׁם. וְכֵיוָן שֶׁמְּצַפֶּה לַאֲחֵרִים חָכְמָתוֹ נִסְרַחַת
וְנַפְשׁוֹ נֶעֱצֶבֶת וּבְשָׂרוֹ עָלָיו יִכְאָב. לֹא כֵן
הַמְקַבֵּל מִיָּדְךָ הַטּוֹבָה הַפְּתוּחָה וְהָרְחָבָה וְהַמְּלֵאָה.
וְלֹא יִצְטָרֵךְ מִן הַבְּרִיּוֹת עַד יוֹם מוֹתוֹ. וּכְשֶׁיִּזְכֶּה
לְזִקְנָה יִהְיֶה רָצוֹן שֶׁלֹּא יָבֹאוּ עָלָיו יִסּוּרִים לֹא כְבֵדִים
וְלֹא קַלִּים וְלֹא יְאָרְעוּ לוֹ חֳלָאִים בְּחַיָּיו. וְתַצִּילֵהוּ
מִכָּל פְּגָעִים וּמִקְרִים רָעִים כְּדֵי שֶׁתָּמִיד יִהְיֶה מוּכָן
לַעֲשׂוֹת רְצוֹנֶךָ. וְתֵן בִּרְצוֹנוֹ לְכַוֵּן לַעֲשׂוֹת רְצוֹנֶךָ. וְאַל
יָבֹא לִידֵי שׁוּם מִכְשׁוֹל דָּבָר שֶׁבָּעוֹלָם לֹא בְּדִבְרֵי
תוֹרָה וְלֹא בְּדִבְרֵי צָרְכּוֹ. וְלֹא יִפּוֹל בּוֹ מוּם מֵחֲמַת
חֳלִי אוֹ מַכָּה וְהַגִּיעֵהוּ לְזִקְנָה בְּבָנִים וּבָנוֹת שֶׁיִּרְאֶה
בְּחֶפְצָן עוֹסְקִים בַּתּוֹרָה וּמִצְוֹת. וְלֹא תִהְיֶה מִיתָתוֹ
מֵחֳלִי כָּבֵד וּמְשֻׁנֶּה. וְיָבֹא אֶל הַקָּדוֹשׁ בָּרוּךְ הוּא
שָׁלֵם בְּכָל־אֵבָרָיו אָמֵן: יִהְיוּ לְרָצוֹן אִמְרֵי פִי וְהֶגְיוֹן
לִבִּי לְפָנֶיךָ יְיָ צוּרִי וְגוֹאֲלִי:

Prayers to Be Recited When She Returns to Synagogue

A prayer of thanksgiving in gratitude to the Lord God because the petitioner has overcome the dangers of birth. It is to be recited by this woman on the Shabbat she returns to the synagogue. She is to recite it with the utmost devotion the moment the Torah is taken out of the Ark.

LORD of the Universe, You hear the prayer of everyone who calls to You, with all their heart and with all their soul; those who fear You and those who tremble before Your word. God, I cannot stop my lips from praising You and thanking You for all the goodness You have shown me, instead of dealing with me as I deserve. What am I? What is my life that You should shed all this goodness and all these miraculous wonders upon me as You have done, God, saving me from the sufferings and travail that accompany pregnancy and childbirth? You continue to grace me with kindness upon kindness, favor and compassion, filling my breasts with milk, enough to feed and nourish this tiny boy (or tiny girl). You have given me the strength to get up from my birthing bed to thank You, and praise You, and exalt Your holy name.

(continued)

Orazione di rendimento di grazie a Dio Signore
per la liberazione del Parto da celebrarsi dalla Donna
in quel שבת , che va a scuola di Parto, e dee dirla
con somma Divozione in quel tempo che è fuori il
ספר תורה .

רִבּוֹן הָעוֹלָמִים אַתָּה שׁוֹמֵעַ תְּפִלַּת כָּל־פֶּה
הַצּוֹעֲקִים אֵלֶיךָ בְּכָל־לְבָבָם וּבְכָל נַפְשָׁם הַיְרֵאִים
וְהַחֲרֵדִים אֶל דְּבָרֶיךָ. יְיָ הִנֵּה שְׂפָתַי לֹא אֶכְלָא
מִלְהוֹדוֹת וּלְשַׁבֵּחַ לְשִׁמְךָ הַגָּדוֹל עַל־כָּל־הַטּוֹבוֹת
שֶׁעָשִׂיתָ עִמָּדִי וְלֹא כִגְמוּלַי הֲשַׁבְתָּנִי. וּמָה אֲנִי וּמָה
חַיַּי שֶׁתַּעֲשֶׂה עִמִּי כַּמָּה גְדוֹלוֹת וְנִסִּים וְנִפְלָאוֹת כְּמוֹ
שֶׁעָשִׂיתָ יְיָ אֱלֹקִים לְהַצִּילֵנִי וּלְמַלְּטֵנִי מִצַּעַר וּמִצִּירֵי
חֶבְלֵי יוֹלֵדָה שֶׁל הֵרָיוֹן שֶׁלִּי. וְעוֹד הוֹסַפְתָּ לִי חֶסֶד
עַל חֶסֶד וְחֶמְלָה וַחֲנִינָה עָלַי לָתֵת לִי חָלָב בְּדַדַּי
שֶׁיַּסְפִּיק לְהַחֲיוֹת וְלָזוּן אֶת הַיֶּלֶד [e se sosse Femmina dirà
(אֶת הַיַּלְדָּה) וְכֹחַ שֶׁיָּכְלְתִּי לַעֲמוֹד מִמִּטָּתִי לְהוֹדוֹת
וּלְשַׁבֵּחַ וּלְכַבֵּד אֶת שִׁמְךָ הַגָּדוֹל.

(continued)

During the time the Temple stood, when we regularly served You through sacrifice, I would have been able to complete Your bidding by bringing the sacrifice You commanded us in Your Torah. And through sacrifice we were forgiven our misdeeds and our mistakes. Now due to our sins and the sins of our ancestors, Jerusalem and Your people are disgraced before the peoples around us. Your Temple, Your pride, is destroyed. We have no altar and no priest to atone for us. Therefore, I rely on Your gracious mercy, for You said You would receive the words of our mouths as if they were sacrifices. As it is written, "We will pay the sacrifice of the bulls with our lips."

Therefore, I pour out my thoughts and my needs before You, and turn to read the Torah portion relating to my sacrifice:

(continued)

וּבִזְמַן שֶׁהָיָה בֵּית הַמִּקְדָּשׁ קַיָּם וְהָיִינוּ
עוֹסְקִים בַּעֲבוֹדָתֶךָ הָיִיתִי יְכוֹלָה לְהַשְׁלִים רְצוֹנְךָ
בְּהַקְרֵב הַקָּרְבָּנוֹת שֶׁצִּוִּיתָנוּ בְּתוֹרָתֶךָ לְהַקְרִיב וּבָהֶם
הָיִינוּ מִתְכַּפְּרִים עַל שִׁגְגוֹתֵינוּ וּזְדוֹנוֹתֵינוּ. וְעַתָּה
בַּעֲוֹנוֹתֵינוּ וַעֲוֹנוֹת אֲבוֹתֵינוּ יְרוּשָׁלַם וְעַמְּךָ לְחֶרְפָּה
לְכָל־סְבִיבוֹתֵינוּ. וּבֵית קָדְשָׁךְ וְתִפְאַרְתְּךָ חָרֵב. וְאֵין
לָנוּ מִזְבֵּחַ וְלֹא כֹהֵן שֶׁיְּכַפֵּר בַּעֲדֵינוּ. לָכֵן נִשְׁעַנְתִּי עַל
רוֹב רַחֲמֶיךָ שֶׁאָמַרְתָּ לְקַבֵּל שִׂיחַ שִׂפְתוֹתֵינוּ
כְּקָרְבָּנוֹת. כְּמוֹ שֶׁכָּתוּב וּנְשַׁלְּמָה פָרִים שְׂפָתֵינוּ.
וְאֶשְׁפּוֹךְ לְפָנֶיךָ שִׂיחִי וְשַׁוְעָתִי וְאֶקְרָא תּוֹרַת קָרְבָּנִי:

(continued)

THE LORD spoke to Moses, saying: Speak to the Israelite people thus: When a woman at childbirth bears a male, she shall be unclean seven days; she shall be unclean as at the time of her menstrual infirmity.—On the eighth day the flesh of his foreskin shall be circumcised.—She shall remain in a state of blood purification for thirty-three days: she shall not touch any consecrated thing, nor enter the sanctuary until her period of purification is completed. If she bears a female, she shall be unclean two weeks as during her menstruation, and she shall remain in a state of blood purification for sixty-six days.

On the completion of her period of purification, for either son or daughter, she shall bring to the priest, at the entrance of the Tent of Meeting, a lamb in its first year for a burnt offering, and a pigeon or a turtledove for a sin offering. He shall offer it before the LORD and make expiation on her behalf; she shall then be clean from her flow of blood. Such are the rituals concerning her who bears a child, male or female. If, however, her means do not suffice for a sheep, she shall take two turtledoves or two pigeons, one for a burnt offering and the other for a sin offering. The priest shall make expiation on her behalf, and she shall be clean.

Leviticus 12:1–8

Relief is hers. Child and mother are fine. The woman returns to the community healthy and whole and it is there that she expresses her gratitude to God. As the walls of the ark open, and the Torah is eased out into the recipient's cradling arms, the woman rejoices that her baby's delivery went well.

Why the need for a sin-offering after birth? And why is the waiting period after the birth of a daughter twice that of a son? Many answers have been sug-

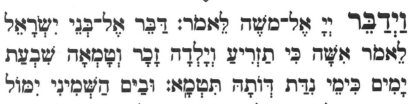

וַיְדַבֵּ֥ר יְיָ אֶל־מֹשֶׁ֖ה לֵּאמֹֽר: דַּבֵּ֞ר אֶל־בְּנֵ֤י יִשְׂרָאֵל֙
לֵאמֹ֔ר אִשָּׁה֙ כִּ֣י תַזְרִ֔יעַ וְיָלְדָ֖ה זָכָ֑ר וְטָֽמְאָה֙ שִׁבְעַ֣ת
יָמִ֔ים כִּימֵ֛י נִדַּ֥ת דְּוֹתָ֖הּ תִּטְמָֽא: וּבַיּ֖וֹם הַשְּׁמִינִ֑י יִמּ֖וֹל
בְּשַׂ֥ר עָרְלָתֽוֹ: וּשְׁלֹשִׁ֥ים יוֹם֙ וּשְׁלֹ֣שֶׁת יָמִ֔ים תֵּשֵׁ֖ב
בִּדְמֵ֣י טָֽהֳרָ֑ה בְּכָל־קֹ֣דֶשׁ לֹֽא־תִגָּ֗ע וְאֶל־הַמִּקְדָּשׁ֙ לֹ֣א
תָבֹ֔א עַד־מְלֹ֖את יְמֵ֥י טָהֳרָֽהּ: וְאִם־נְקֵבָ֣ה תֵלֵ֔ד וְטָֽמְאָ֥ה
שְׁבֻעַ֖יִם כְּנִדָּתָ֑הּ וְשִׁשִּׁ֥ים יוֹם֙ וְשֵׁ֣שֶׁת יָמִ֔ים תֵּשֵׁ֖ב
עַל־דְּמֵ֥י טָהֳרָֽה: וּבִמְלֹ֣את ׀ יְמֵ֣י טָהֳרָ֗הּ לְבֵן֙ א֣וֹ לְבַ֔ת
תָּבִ֞יא כֶּ֤בֶשׂ בֶּן־שְׁנָתוֹ֙ לְעֹלָ֔ה וּבֶן־יוֹנָ֥ה אֽוֹ־תֹ֖ר לְחַטָּ֑את
אֶל־פֶּ֥תַח אֹֽהֶל־מוֹעֵ֖ד אֶל־הַכֹּהֵֽן: וְהִקְרִיב֞וֹ לִפְנֵ֤י יְיָ֙
וְכִפֶּ֣ר עָלֶ֔יהָ וְטָהֲרָ֖ה מִמְּקֹ֣ר דָּמֶ֑יהָ זֹ֤את תּוֹרַת֙ הַיֹּלֶ֔דֶת
לַזָּכָ֖ר א֣וֹ לַנְּקֵבָֽה: וְאִם־לֹ֨א תִמְצָ֣א יָדָהּ֮ דֵּ֣י שֶׂה֒ וְלָֽקְחָ֣ה
שְׁתֵּֽי־תֹרִ֗ים א֤וֹ שְׁנֵי֙ בְּנֵ֣י יוֹנָ֔ה אֶחָ֥ד לְעֹלָ֖ה וְאֶחָ֣ד
לְחַטָּ֑את וְכִפֶּ֥ר עָלֶ֛יהָ הַכֹּהֵ֖ן וְטָהֵֽרָה:

---

gested. One, from tradition, suggests that the sacrifice is to atone for the harsh words the woman may have uttered during childbirth. A modern attempt suggests that the sin offering atones for the woman coming too close to, or mimick-ing too convincingly, the act of creation, a unique attribute of God. And since a daughter bears within her the seeds of an identical transgression, the time of impurity after the birth of a girl—although not the sacrifice itself—is doubled.

NOW, I trust in Your words. I hold my life in the palm of my hands and beseech You, Lord of all the world, the one and only God, the one and only Lord, the highest of the high, Who sits among the heavens, surveying all below. God upon high, in Your great goodness and mercy, may You take my words and gather my prayers and petitions and pleas that come from the very bottom of my heart. Gather them willingly unto You. Receive them instead of the sacrifices I would have been obliged to offer (in days of old). May You deem them as sweet-smelling incense before You. May You always be with me and continually give me strength and courage. Also, give my husband the stamina and ability to raise this new child [and if there are other children: along with our other children] so that we may be spared the pains of parenthood. Let us raise them with our values and our desire to serve You and to love You and to do Your bidding without reservation and with a pure heart. May these words, which I utter before You, be as righteous sacrifices, as a pleasing aroma. Amen. Selah.

Do this for Your name's sake, the sake of Your right hand, the sake of Your Torah and Your holiness. May the words of my mouth and the meditations of my heart be acceptable to You, my Rock and my Redeemer.

Conclusion of this prayer

From the time of the destruction of the Temple, when sacrifices necessarily ceased, until this very day, prayer—the service of the heart—has been seen as a substitute, a surrogate, for the sacrificial offerings. To some, prayer surpassed sacrifice as a way to approach God. To others, prayer is simply the best possible alternative. This prayer seems to favor the latter view.

Even more potent than simply substituting words for sacrifice is the recitation of the description of the sacrifices as found in the Torah. If we cannot perform

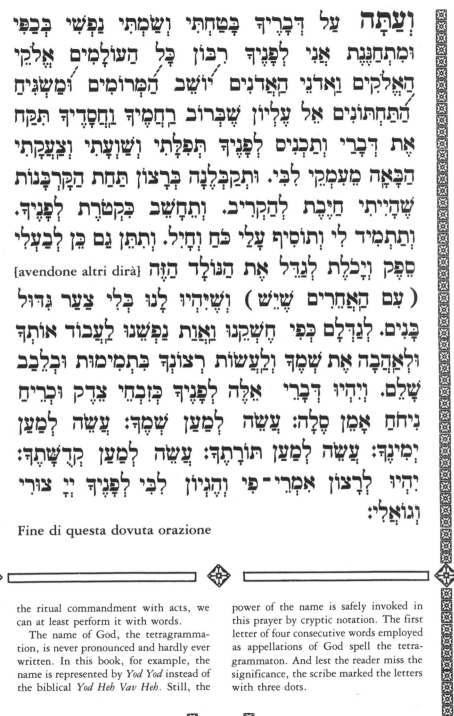

וְעַתָּה עַל דְּבָרֶיךָ בָּטַחְתִּי וְשַׂמְתִּי נַפְשִׁי בְכַפִּי
וּמִתְחַנֶּנֶת אֲנִי לְפָנֶיךָ רִבּוֹן כָּל הָעוֹלָמִים אֱלֹקֵי
הָאֱלֹקִים וַאדֹנֵי הָאֲדֹנִים יוֹשֵׁב הַמְּרוֹמִים וּמַשְׁגִּיחַ
הַתַּחְתּוֹנִים אֵל עֶלְיוֹן שֶׁבָּרוֹב בְּרַחֲמֶיךָ וַחֲסָדֶיךָ תִּקַּח
אֶת דְּבָרַי וְתַכְנִים לְפָנֶיךָ תְּפִלָּתִי וְשַׁוְעָתִי וְצַעֲקָתִי
הַבָּאָה מֵעִמְקֵי לִבִּי. וּתְקַבְּלֶנָּה בְּרָצוֹן תַּחַת הַקָּרְבָּנוֹת
שֶׁהָיִיתִי חַיֶּבֶת לְהַקְרִיב. וְתַחֲשָׁב כִּקְטֹרֶת לְפָנֶיךָ.
וְתַתְמִיד לִי וְתוֹסִיף עָלַי כֹּחַ וָחָיִל. וְתִתֵּן גַּם כֵּן לְבַעְלִי
[avendone altri dirà] סֶפֶק וִכֹלֶת לְגַדֵּל אֶת הַנּוֹלָד הַזֶּה
(עִם הָאֲחֵרִים שֶׁיֵּשׁ) וְשֶׁיִּהְיוּ לָנוּ בְּלִי צַעַר גָּדוֹל
בָּנִים. לְגַדְּלָם כְּפִי חֶשְׁקֵנוּ וְאַוַּת נַפְשֵׁנוּ לַעֲבוֹד אוֹתְךָ
וּלְאַהֲבָה אֶת שְׁמֶךָ וְלַעֲשׂוֹת רְצוֹנְךָ בִּתְמִימוּת וּבְלֵבָב
שָׁלֵם. וְיִהְיוּ דְבָרַי אֵלֶּה לְפָנֶיךָ כְּזִבְחֵי צֶדֶק וּכְרֵיחַ
נִיחֹחַ אָמֵן סֶלָה: עֲשֵׂה לְמַעַן שְׁמֶךָ: עֲשֵׂה לְמַעַן
יְמִינֶךָ: עֲשֵׂה לְמַעַן תּוֹרָתֶךָ: עֲשֵׂה לְמַעַן קְדֻשָּׁתֶךָ:
יִהְיוּ לְרָצוֹן אִמְרֵי - פִי וְהֶגְיוֹן לִבִּי לְפָנֶיךָ יְיָ צוּרִי
וְגוֹאֲלִי:

Fine di questa dovuta orazione

the ritual commandment with acts, we can at least perform it with words.

The name of God, the tetragrammation, is never pronounced and hardly ever written. In this book, for example, the name is represented by *Yod Yod* instead of the biblical *Yod Heh Vav Heh*. Still, the power of the name is safely invoked in this prayer by cryptic notation. The first letter of four consecutive words employed as appellations of God spell the tetragrammaton. And lest the reader miss the significance, the scribe marked the letters with three dots.

Prayer to Be Recited
When One Assists in Childbirth

When a woman attends at the birth of a friend's child she must show great devotion. She cannot allow trivial conversation or an obscene or malicious word. Her task must always be directed toward giving courage to the woman in labor and to assisting her, and at the same time exhorting her to put her trust in God, to place all her hope only in God. She must also encourage her to say the confessional prayer. The woman in labor must be released from all her vows; she should now make a vow to perform some mitzvah, *for example, spinning wool for* tzitzit, *making wicks for use in the synagogue, washing* tallitot, *or being punctilious in observing* Rosh Hodesh, *or some other similar tasks pertaining to women. Then the attendant woman says the following prayer on behalf of the woman in labor:*

Quando una Donna va ad assistere al Parto di una
qualche sua amica, dee stare ivi con grande divozione,
ne permettere mai che in sua prefenza sifacciano
discorsi vani, e molto meno osceni, o maliziosi, ma la
sua mira dee sempre essere diretta a tenere in
coniggio la Partoriente, ad assisterla, e nello stesso
tempo ad esortarla di ricorrere a Dio, e di riporre
in lui solo ogni di lei speranza. Dee pure consigliarla
a dire il וידוי , e a farsi fare התרת נדרים וקללות ,
e ad assumersi un qualche נדר per l'esecuzione di
qualche מצוה ; come per esempio di filare lana per
farne ציצית , o di fare stupini per uso del בית הכנסת ;
o di lavare טליתות ; o di essere esatta nell'
osservare il ראש חדש ; o altre cose simili
appartenenti a donne: E poi dirà a favore de
la Partoriente la seguente תפלה .

MAY IT BE Your will, great and exalted God, that I not cause any misfortune. May You remember the meritorious deeds of this humble woman, this woman who will moan and cry in the midst of her labor, whose cries will rise before Your holy throne. Silence those who speak against her and gather before You those who speak well of her, as You do for those deserving and those undeserving. May You always be merciful with her, for You respond in times of need, King of Mercy, the One who is merciful to all, who redeems and saves and listens and answers. Amen.

Conclusion

Reference is again made here to a court-room scene where the woman's voice is raised in her own defense against those who seize this moment to speak against her. The danger of death that accompanies childbirth is acknowledged by the recitation of the personal confession and the release from all vows. Yet, to assure

יְהִי רָצוֹן מִלְפָנֶיךָ הַשֵׁם הַגָּדוֹל הַגִּבּוֹר וְהַנּוֹרָא שֶׁלֹּא
תָבֹא שׁוּם תַּקָלָה עַל יָדִי וְיִזָּכְרוּ לְפָנֶיךָ זְכִיּוֹת הָאִשָּׁה
הָעֲנִיָּה הַזֹּאת אֲשֶׁר תָּחִיל תִּצְעַק בַּחֲבָלֶיהָ וְתַעֲלֶה קוֹל
צַעֲקָתָה עַד כִּסֵּא כְבוֹדֶךָ. וּסְתוֹם פִּי הַמְקַטְרְגִים עָלֶיהָ
וִיכָּנְסוּ לְפָנֶיךָ כָּל־הַמְּלִיצִים בַּעֲדָה טוֹב. כְּמִדָּתְךָ
לְהֵיטִיב לָהֲגוּן וּלְבִלְתִּי הָגוּן. וְיִכְמְרוּ רַחֲמֶיךָ עָלֶיהָ. כִּי
אַתָּה עוֹנֶה בְּעֵת צָרָה מֶלֶךְ רַחֲמָן וּמְרַחֵם עַל כָּל
פּוֹדֶה וּמַצִּיל שׁוֹמֵעַ וְעוֹנֶה: אָמֵן:

Fine

her well-being, the petitioner also assumes an obligation to be fulfilled after
she has safely given birth. This vow is
directed to a task that devolves upon

women. A woman's task threatens her; a
woman's task can save her.

127